The Young People's Picture Dictionary

Anne Scott

Illustrated by Tony Kenyon

Oliver & Boyd

Author's photograph by David Grant
Cover illustration by John Lobban

Oliver & Boyd
Robert Stevenson House
1 – 3 Baxter's Place
Leith Walk
Edinburgh EH1 3BB

A Division of Longman Group UK Ltd

ISBN 0 05 004375 7

First published 1990

© Oliver & Boyd 1990

All rights reserved; no part of this publication
may be reproduced, stored in a retrieval system,
or transmitted in any form or by any means,
electronic, mechanical, photocopying, recording,
or otherwise, without either the prior written permission
of the Publishers or a licence permitting
restricted copying issued by the Copyright Licensing
Agency Ltd, 33 – 34 Alfred Place, London, WC1E 7DP.

Set in Linotron Optima 12 on 13pt
Produced by Longman Group (FE) Ltd
Printed in Hong Kong

The Young Person's Picture Dictionary

A a

about   Fairy tales are *about* magic things.   They tell of fairies and giants and wishes that come true.

About also means this way and that way and all over the place.   You run *about* in a game of chase.

above   Your nose is *above* your mouth. It is higher.   *Above* is on top.   Jack's beanstalk grew and grew till it was high *above* the clouds.

absent   *Absent* is not here.   *Absent* means away.   An *absent* schoolboy is not in class.

accident   Something that happens when you do not think it will happen is an *accident*.   An *accident* happens by chance.

Oops! **Accidents** do happen!

ache   A pain that hurts for quite a long time is an *ache*, like *toothache*.

acorn   An *acorn* is the nut of an oak tree.   An *acorn* looks like a little egg in a little eggcup.

acrobat   An *acrobat* swings and tumbles and walks a tightrope at the circus.

across   From one side to the other side is *across*.   Walk safely *across* the road at the crossing.

act   To *act* is to do something, anything at all.   An *act* is something that you do.

To *act* is also to pretend, or play at being someone else in a show or a play.

add   You put things together when you *add*.
Add 2 pence and 3 pence to have 5 pence.
Add boiling water to a tea bag to have tea.

address   Your *address* is where you live; your number, your street and your town or your village.

adult   A child grows up to be an *adult*.   An *adult* is a grownup.

adventure   Exciting and sometimes frightening things happen in an *adventure*.
Jack's *adventures* began when he climbed the beanstalk.

aerial   An *aerial* is a wire or rod that brings pictures or sound to a television or radio.

aeroplane   An *aeroplane* is a machine that flies through the air.

afraid   Was Goldilocks *afraid* of the Three Bears?
   Yes, she was so frightened she ran and ran.

after   Night comes *after* day.   It is later. The giant came down the beanstalk *after* Jack. He was right behind.

afternoon   The time between 12 o'clock noon, and evening is *afternoon*.

again   *Again* is more than once or often. Jack climbed the beanstalk *again* and *again*.   He climbed it three times.

against   *Against* is touching or leaning, like a ladder *against* a wall.

   Against also means opposite or on different sides.
   Scotland plays football *against* England.

age   What *age* are you? How old are you? How many birthdays have you had?

ago   *Ago* means at a time that has gone past?
   Many years *ago* dinosaurs lived on the Earth.

aim   To *aim* is to point at a target before trying to hit it.

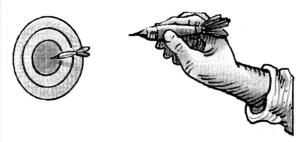

air   *Air* is everywhere around you, to breathe in and keep you alive.

aircraft   *Aircraft* are all kinds of aeroplanes.
   An *airline steward or stewardess* looks after passengers in an aeroplane.   *Aircraft* take off and land at an *airport*.

album   An *album* is a book to keep special collections of things together.   Photographs, stamps, dried flowers and lots of other things can be put into an *album*.

alive   *Alive* is living and breathing and full of life.   *Alive* is not dead.

all *All* is not just some. *All* is the whole of a thing. *All* is everything and everybody.

alligator An *alligator* is an animal that lives in and near rivers in hot lands. An *alligator* has strong jaws and sharp teeth. It looks like a small crocodile but its nose is shorter and broader.

allow To *allow* is to let someone do something.
Cinderella's wicked stepmother did not *allow* her to go to the ball, but her fairy godmother said she could go.

almost *Almost* means very nearly. At one minute to 12 noon it is *almost* noon.

alone You are *alone* when nobody else is with you. You are by yourself.

along Dick Whittington set off *along* the road to London. He walked all the way.

aloud You can be heard when you speak *aloud*. You are not speaking in a whisper.

alphabet The *alphabet* is all the letters from A to Z. There are 26 letters in the *alphabet*.

already *Already* means by this time or before the time.
The Little Pig had *already* been to the apple orchard before the time the wolf got there.

Already also means so soon. Is it bedtime *already*?

also *Also* is too or as well. Jack is a boy. Tom is *also* a boy.

always Every time and for ever and ever is *always*.

ambulance An *ambulance* is a big car that takes sick people quickly to hospital.

among   *Among* means in the middle of. A little cottage was hidden *among* the trees.

Among also means to each one of. Divide 8 fish *among* 4 cats and each one will have 2 fish.

anchor   An *anchor* is a big, strong, heavy hook at the end of a chain.   When it is dropped from a ship it fastens onto the sea bottom and stops the ship moving.

angry   Jack's mother was *angry* when he sold the cow for a bag of beans. She was very cross and bad-tempered.

animal   An *animal* is any living thing that moves.   It can be a lion or a mouse, a fish or a snake, a bird or a bee.

ankle   Your *ankle* is the part of your leg above your foot.

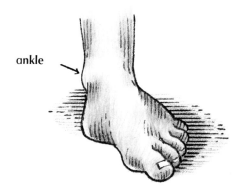

ankle

annual   *Annual* means happening once a year, like your birthday.

An *annual* is also a book that comes out once a year.

anorak   An *anorak* is a warm waterproof jacket.   An *anorak* usually has a hood.

another   *Another* means different or not the same.
The first Little Pig went one way.   The second Little Pig went *another* way.   The third Little Pig went *another* way.   They all took different ways.

Another also means one more.
Red Riding Hood picked a flower for her grandmother.   Then *another* and *another* and *another*.   She picked one more each time.

answer   An *answer* is what you say or write when you are asked a question.
'Where are you going?' the wolf asked.
'To visit my grandmother,' was Red Riding Hood's *answer*.

ant   An *ant* is a very small, very busy insect.   It lives and works with lots of other *ants*.

anything   *Anything* means one thing or something or whatever.

apple   An *apple* is a round fruit with red or green or yellow skin.
The Little Pig got to the *apple* orchard before the wolf.

April   *April* is the fourth month of the year.   It has 30 days.

apron   An *apron* is a piece of cloth or plastic to tie round your waist and over your clothes to keep them clean.

aquarium   You can see fish and water plants in an *aquarium*.   Usually it is a big glass tank full of water.

arch   An *arch* is a curved shape like a rainbow.
In buildings you may see an *arch* over a door, a window or a gateway.   Some bridges are *arched*.

ark   The *ark* was the big boat Noah built before the flood.   The *ark* held his family and two of every kind of animal.

In the Bible an *ark* was also a box or a chest.

arm   Your *arm* is between your shoulder and your hand.
You can rest your *arms* on the sides of an *armchair*.

army   An *army* is a large number of soldiers.

arrive   You *arrive* when you come to the place where you want to be.
Dick Whittington walked many miles before he *arrived* in London.

arrow   An *arrow* is a long thin stick with a sharp tip shot from a bow at a target.

artist   An *artist* draws or paints pictures.

ash   When a fire burns away, all that is left is soft grey *ash*.

ask   If you want to know something you *ask* a question.

asleep   The giant was *asleep* when Jack ran off with his magic hen.   He was not awake.

astronaut   An *astronaut* travels into space in a spaceship.

atlas   An *atlas* is a book of maps.

audience   People who listen to a concert or a talk or go to see a play or a film are the *audience*.

August   *August* is the eighth month of the year.   It has 31 days.

aunt   Your *aunt* is the sister of your mother or your father.

autumn   *Autumn* is the season of the year when fruit is ripe on the fruit trees and leaves begin to fall. In some countries this season is called the fall.

avalanche   When lots of snow and ice come tumbling down the mountainside it is an *avalanche*.

awake   When the giant's magic hen cackled loudly, the giant was quickly *awake*.   He was no longer asleep.

away   You are not here when you are *away*.   You are somewhere else.

axe   Jack took the *axe* by its long handle and with its sharp blade he chopped down the beanstalk.

B b

baby A *baby* is a very young child. *Babies* cannot talk or walk yet.

back The *back* of anything is behind and not in front. You can carry a schoolbag on your *back*.

bacon *Bacon* is salty meat from the pig.

bad *Bad* is not good, like the wicked wolf Red Riding Hood met in the wood.

Red Riding Hood meets the big **bad** wolf.

badge A *badge* is a special mark or sign or pin to wear to show you are at a school or in a club.

bag A *bag* opens at the top and holds or carries all kinds of things. It can be made of paper or cloth or leather or plastic.

bake To *bake* is to cook food in an oven. A *baker* makes and *bakes* bread, buns, pies and cakes in his *bakery*.

bald A *bald* head has no hair on it.

ball A *ball* is round and soft or hard for playing games. You can throw it or hit it or bounce it or kick it.

A *ball* is also a grand dance held in a *ballroom*.

balloon A little bag of thin rubber blows up into a big, bouncing, floating *balloon*.

banana A *banana* is a long, thin, curved fruit with a thick yellow skin.

band A *band* is people playing music together for listening to or for dancers to dance to.

A *band* goes round things to keep them in place, like an elastic *band* or a *hairband*.

bandage A *bandage* is a strip of cloth to cover and tie round a cut on your skin.

bank Your money is kept safe for you in a *bank*.

The sides of a river are called the *banks*.

bar A *bar* is a long piece of wood or metal like one of the *bars* on a gate, or an iron *bar* or a *bar* of gold.

A *bar* is also a counter where food and drinks are sold.

barbecue A *barbecue* is a special grill used for cooking food out of doors.   When you eat food cooked like this you are having a *barbecue*.

barber A *barber* cuts men's and boys' hair and shaves men's faces.

bark The noise a dog makes is its *bark*.

The *bark* of a tree is its rough outside skin.

barn On the farm a *barn* is a large building for keeping hay and crops or animals.

barrel A *barrel* is a big, round wooden tub with strong rings of metal to hold it together.   Water or oil or beer can be kept in a *barrel*.

basket Red Riding Hood filled a *basket* with good things for her grandmother. Her *basket* was made of thick, twisted straw and had a handle.

bat A *bat* is a piece of wood for hitting the ball in some games.   A cricket *bat* is not the same shape as a table tennis *bat*.

A *bat* is also an animal like a mouse with wings.

bath   A *bath* is a long tub you can step into and wash all of your body.   It is kept in the *bathroom*.

battery   A *battery* stores electricity. Lots of electric things like torches, radios, clocks and calculators use *batteries* to make them work.

battle   A *battle* is a fight in a war between armies, ships or aeroplanes.

bay   A *bay* is part of the sea or a lake that curves into the land.

beach   The *beach* is the sand or pebbles along the edge of the sea or a lake.

bead   A *bead* is a small piece of glass or stone or wood with a hole in it.   You string lots of *beads* together to make a necklace.

beak   A bird pecks with its *beak*.   A *beak* is the hard and pointed part of its mouth.

bean   A *bean* is a vegetable with seeds that grow in pods.
   Jack's magic *beanstalk* grew and grew.

bear   A *bear* is a big wild animal.   Its fur is brown or white or black.
   The Three Bears Goldilocks met were brown *bears*.

beard   The hair that grows on a man's face is his *beard*.

beat   To *beat* is to strike hard.   A drummer *beats* his drum with a drumstick.

   To *beat* also means to win or come first in a race or a battle.

beautiful   Snow White was the most *beautiful* girl in all the land.   She was very, very pretty.

because   *Because* tells you the reason for something.   *Because* tells you why.
   Why could the wolf not blow down the Little Pig's house?
   Because it was built with bricks. That is why.

bed   A *bed* is nice to lie down and sleep on, with a pillow for your head and covers to keep you warm.   A *bed* is kept in the *bedroom*.

bee   A *bee* is an insect that flies from flower to flower.   It has black and yellow stripes and can make honey.   A *bee* can sting.

beef   *Beef* is meat from cows and bulls.

beetle   A *beetle* is an insect with a hard skin and wings.

before   *Before* is earlier and not later. Who got to the apple orchard *before* the wolf?

Before is in front of and not behind.

begin   To *begin* is to start.   When you *begin* to read a story you start at the *beginning*.

behave   To *behave* is to do or to act. To *behave* well is to be good.   To be on your best *behaviour* is to be very good and polite.

behind   *Behind* is at the back of and not in front.

Cinderella sat in a glass coach *behind* six white horses.

believe   To *believe* is to think a thing is true.   To *believe* is to think someone is telling the truth.

bell   A *bell* looks like an upside down cup made of metal.

A *bell* rings if you strike it or shake it.   Some *bells* are electric and ring or buzz when you push a button.

belong   Does this book *belong* to you? Is it your own book?   Or does it *belong* to somebody else?

below   *Below* is under or underneath. Your chin is *below* your mouth.

belt   A *belt* is a band of leather or cloth or plastic to wear round your waist.

bend   To *bend* is to curve, like your back when you *bend* to tie your shoes. Your back is not straight when you *bend*.   It is *bent*.

berry   A *berry* is a small, juicy fruit with seeds inside.   You can eat some *berries*.

Do you like *strawberries* or *raspberries*?

strawberries

raspberries

beside   *Beside* is close to or near. *Beside* is side by side.

best   Nothing is better than *best*.   *Best* is not just good. It is very, very good. The *best* runner comes first in the race.

better   *Better* is more than good but not so good as best.

between   *Between* your eyes and your mouth is your nose.   Your nose is in the middle.

Big Daddy Bear rides the biggest **bicycle**.

bicycle   A *bicycle* has two wheels and two pedals to make the wheels go round.

big   *Big* is large like Daddy Bear.   He was *bigger* than Mummy Bear and Baby Bear.   He was the *biggest* bear.

bird   A *bird* is an animal with wings and feathers and two legs.   Most *birds* can fly and all *birds* lay eggs.

birthday   The day you were born is your *birthday*.   On the same day every year you are one year older.

biscuit   A *biscuit* is a small, thin, hard cake baked in the oven.   *Biscuits* are sweet or plain, salty or cheesy.

bit   A small piece is a *bit*.   A *bit* of biscuit is not a whole biscuit.

bite   You take a bit out of something when you *bite* it with your teeth.   The wicked queen made Snow White take a *bite* out of the bad half of the apple.

black   *Black* is very dark like the night sky when there is no moon or stars.

blackberry   A *blackberry* is a small, juicy, shiny black fruit growing on a bush.   *Blackberries* are also called brambles.

blackbird   A *blackbird* has black feathers and a bright yellow beak.

blackboard   A *blackboard* is a piece of smooth, dark board or slate for writing on with chalks.

blade   The *blade* of a knife is the sharp part that cuts things.

A leaf of grass is also called a *blade*.

blanket   A *blanket* is a woolly cover on a bed to keep you warm.

blood   *Blood* is the red liquid pumped by your heart to every part of your body to keep you alive.

blouse   A girl or a woman wears a *blouse* on the top part of her body.

blow   'I'll huff and I'll puff and I'll *blow* your house down,' said the wolf.   He *blew* air out of his mouth as hard as he could.

A *blow* is also a very hard knock.

blue *Blue* is the colour of a sunny sky. *Blue* is the colour of a *bluebell* flower.

board A *board* is a piece of wood that is long and flat.

You step onto a ship or an aeroplane or a train when you *board* it.

boat A *boat* is a small ship that sails on the water.

A *speedboat* goes faster than a *rowing boat*.

body Your *body* is the whole of you from your head to your toes.

boil When you *boil* water you heat it till it bubbles and steams. It is as hot as it can be.

bone A *bone* is a hard white part inside your body. Your *bones* hold your body together underneath your skin.

book Pages of paper fastened together inside a cover make a *book*. On the pages are words to read or pictures to look at.

A *bookcase* is a case with shelves to hold *books*.

boot A *boot* covers your foot and your ankle and sometimes part of your leg.

Puss-in-Boots wore fine leather *boots*.

Do you wear *Wellington boots* when it rains?

born The day you were *born* was the first day of your life. It was your birthday.

borrow To *borrow* is to ask for something you will give back again.

both *Both* is not just one but two. Cinderella had two ugly stepsisters. *Both* of them were ugly.

bottle A *bottle* holds liquids like water and milk and juice and sauce. *Bottles* are usually made of glass or plastic with a cap or a top or a stopper to keep them closed.

bottom The lowest part is the *bottom*. The *bottom* is at the foot of anything. Jack started at the *bottom* of the beanstalk and climbed to the top.

bounce To spring or jump up and down is to *bounce*, like a *bouncing* rubber ball.

bow (This *bow* rhymes with toe.)
A *bow* is a knot with loops. You can tie ribbon in a *bow*, or your shoe laces in a *bow*, or a *bow tie* in a *bow*.

A *bow* is also a wooden weapon that bends into a curve to shoot arrows.

bow (This *bow* rhymes with cow.)
Bow means to bend your head or your body politely. An actor *bows* when the audience claps.

With **bows** on his toes, a **bow tie** round his neck, an actor takes his **bow**.

bowl A *bowl* is a round deep dish that holds things. A *soup bowl* holds soup, a *fruit bowl* holds fruit.
Goldilocks ate up all the porridge in Baby Bear's *porridge bowl*.

box A *box* can hold almost anything. It has straight sides, sometimes has a lid and is made of wood or cardboard or metal.

boxer A *boxer* fights with his fists. He wears *boxing gloves* made of leather.

boy A *boy* is a child who will be a man when he is older.

bracelet A *bracelet* is a band or a chain to wear round your wrist or your arm.

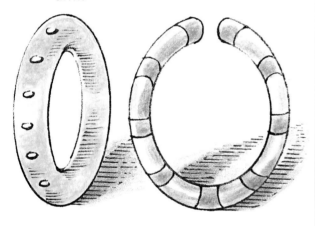

brake The *brake* is part of a car or any machine that makes it go slower or stops it.

branch A *branch* of a tree grows like an arm from its trunk. *Branches* are covered in leaves in spring and summer.

brave To be *brave* is to show no fear. You are not afraid.

bread *Bread* is food made mostly of flour. A baker bakes *bread* in an oven.

break To *break* is to smash like an egg if you drop it.
Goldilocks was too heavy for Baby Bear's chair and she *broke* it.

breakfast *Breakfast* is eaten in the morning. It is the first meal of the day.

breath The air you take into your body and blow out again is your *breath*. You *breathe* it in and out through your nose.

brick A *brick* is a block of clay and sand baked until it is hard.
The third Little Pig built his house with lots of *bricks* stuck together.

bride A woman is a *bride* on her wedding day. A man is a *bridegroom* on his wedding day.
Cinderella was the *bride* and the prince was the *bridegroom* on their wedding day.

bridge A *bridge* is built to let you cross over a river or a railway or a road.

bright *Bright* is shining like light. *Bright* is sunny and cheerful. *Bright* is full of colour like a *bright* blue sky.

bring   To *bring* is to fetch or to carry. '*Bring* me a pumpkin,' said the fairy godmother.   And Cinderella *brought* one from the garden.

broad   *Broad* is wide from one side to the other.   A motorway is a *broad* road.   It is not narrow.

brother   If you have a *brother*, he is a boy with the same mother and father as you.

brown   *Brown* is the colour of chocolate, the earth, and dead leaves.

brush   Strong hairs or soft hairs fixed to a handle make a *brush*.   *Brushes* are for cleaning or sweeping or painting or to tidy your hair.

bubble   A very thin ball of liquid full of air or gas is a *bubble*.

bucket   A *bucket* is a pail.   It holds water and has a handle to carry it.

buckle   A *buckle* fastens the two ends of a belt or a strap.   Some shoes have *buckles*.

bud   A *bud* is a flower or a leaf before it opens out.

build   To make things is to *build*.   A *builder* joins things together to make *buildings*, like houses or towers or factories.
   The third Little Pig *built* his house with bricks.

Which Little Pig **built** his house with **bricks**?

17

bulb Some flowers grow from a *bulb*. It is a round root like an onion. Daffodils and tulips grow from *bulbs*.

A *bulb* is also the glass round an electric light.

bull A *bull* is the male of a cow, an elephant or a whale.

bulldozer A *bulldozer* is a large heavy tractor. It has a very strong blade at the front to move loads of earth and rocks.

bullet A small piece of metal to shoot from a gun is a *bullet*.

bump To knock or hit against is to *bump*.

bunch Red Riding Hood picked some flowers for her grandmother. She put them all together in a *bunch*.

buoy A *buoy* marks dangerous rocks or shallow water. It floats on the sea but is fixed under the water.

burglar A thief who breaks into buildings to steal is a *burglar*.

burn To be in flames or on fire is to *burn*.

burst To break with a pop or a bang is to *burst*, like a balloon you have blown up too hard.

bury When you put something or hide something in the ground you *bury* it. Pirates *buried* treasure.

bus A *bus* travels on the road. It has lots of seats, and stops for you at the *bus stop*.

bush A *bush* is a small, low tree with many branches. Roses grow on a *rosebush*. Raspberries grow on a *raspberry bush*.

busy You are *busy* when you have lots to do.

butcher A *butcher* cuts up meat to sell in his *butcher's shop*.

butter *Butter* is soft and yellow and you can spread it on bread. *Butter* is a food made from cream.

butterfly A *butterfly* is an insect with four pretty wings.

button A *button* fastens two sides of your clothes together. It is a little knob or disc that slides into a *buttonhole*.

buy You give money for something when you *buy*.
Dick Whittington *bought* his cat with his first pay.

C c

cabbage A *cabbage* is a vegetable with thick green or red leaves. You can eat it cooked or raw.

café You can eat light meals in a *café*.

cage Birds or animals are sometimes kept in a *cage*. A *cage* has bars or wire round it.

cake A *cake* is soft and sweet, made with flour and sugar and eggs and baked in the oven. *Cakes* are sometimes baked for special days like a *birthday cake* or a *wedding cake*.

calculator A machine that helps you to count is a *calculator*.

calendar A *calendar* is a list of all the days and dates in every month of the year.

calf A *calf* is a young cow or bull or elephant or whale.

call To *call* is to give a name to somebody. What are you *called*? What is your name?

Call is also to cry out or shout.

camel A *camel* is a big strong animal with one or two humps on its back. *Camels* carry heavy loads on long journeys across the hot desert. They can travel a long way without food and water.

camera A *camera* is a machine that takes photographs or films.

camp You sleep in a tent in the open air when you *camp*. *Campers* cook food over a *camp fire* or on a *camp stove*.

Click! The **camper's camera** catches the **camel's** smile.

can   A *can* is made of thin metal.   *Cans* are tins and hold all kinds of food and drink, from beans to soup, from sardines to juice.   Paint and petrol are kept in big *cans*.

Can also means you know how to do something.

Can also means to let or be allowed to do something.

candle   A candle is a stick of wax, long or short, fat or thin, with a string called a wick down the middle. The wick burns to give *candlelight*. You have *candles* on a birthday cake, one for every year.

canoe   A *canoe* is a long narrow boat. A paddle sends it gliding through the water.

cap   A *cap* is a small, soft hat that fits close to your head.

A *cap* is also a lid on a bottle or a tube.

captain   A ship and an aeroplane and a games team all have a *captain*.   He or she is the person in charge.   A *captain* is also an officer in the army.

car   You drive by road in a *car*.   Most *cars* have four wheels and they all have a wheel inside to steer with.

caravan   A *caravan* is a little house on wheels.   It can be pulled by a car.

card   A *card* is a piece of strong paper.   You can write on some cards like *Christmas cards* or *postcards*.   You play games with *playing cards*.

cardboard   *Cardboard* is made of stronger and thicker paper than a card.   Boxes can be made of *cardboard*.

cardigan   A *cardigan* is a woolly jacket with buttons.

care   You watch out when you take *care*.   You are *careful*.

Care also means to look after and be good to someone.
   The Seven Dwarfs *cared* for Snow White.

carol   A *carol* is a song of joy to sing at Christmas.

carpenter   A *carpenter* makes things out of wood with a saw, a hammer and nails.

carpet   A *carpet* is a covering for a floor.   It is thick and soft to walk on.

carrot   A *carrot* is a long vegetable with a pointed end.   It is orange-red and you can eat it cooked or raw.

carry   You *carry* school books from home to school.   You take them from one place to another.
  The glass coach *carried* Cinderella to the ball.

cartoon   A funny drawing is a *cartoon*.   A film made with drawings is a *cartoon* too, like *101 Dalmatians*.

case   A *case* is a box for holding things and for carrying things.   A *suitcase* holds and carries your clothes.

cassette   A *cassette* is a little plastic box that holds music tapes and speaking tapes to play in a *cassette recorder*. *Videocassettes* hold films.

castle   A *castle* is a big old building with thick stone walls and towers. *Castles* were built long ago to keep out enemies.

cat   A *cat* is a small animal with thick, soft fur and whiskers.   *Cats* are good pets.
  Some *cats* like Dick Whittington's *cat* are kept to catch mice.

catch   Cats *catch* mice, boys and girls *catch* balls, fishermen *catch* fish. They get hold of things that are moving.
  Jack was too quick for the giant and he did not get *caught*.

caterpillar   A *caterpillar* looks like a little worm and grows into a butterfly.

cave   A *cave* is a large hole under the ground or in the rocks or in a hillside.   Long ago *cavepeople* lived in *caves*.

In the rocks below the **castle** is a **cave**.

ceiling   The roof or the top part of a room is the *ceiling*.

cellar   The *cellar* in a building is a room under the ground to store things, like coal or wine.

centre   The *centre* is the middle.

cereal   *Cereal* is food that comes from grasses with seeds you can eat. Wheat, oats, rice and barley are *cereals*.   Breakfast *cereals* are made from these.

chain   Rings of metal joined together make a *chain*.

chair   A *chair* is a seat for one person with a back and four legs. *Armchairs* have arms too.

chalk   *Chalk* is a soft white rock.   You can draw with *chalk* and write on a blackboard with sticks of *chalk*.

chance   You do not know something will happen when it happens by *chance*.   *Chance* is just luck.

change   When things *change* they are different.   Traffic lights *change* colour.   They are not always the same colour.

You wear different clothes when you *change*.

If you give too much money when you buy, the money you get back is your *change*.

chase   To run after is to *chase*. The giant *chased* Jack.

cheap   If you buy something *cheap* you do not spend very much money.   It is not very dear.

cheek   You have a *cheek* on each side of your face.   Your *cheeks* are between your nose and your ears.

cheese   *Cheese* is a food made from milk.

cherry   A *cherry* is a small round, red fruit with a stone in the middle. *Cherries* grow on *cherry trees*.

chest   A *chest* is a big strong box with a lid.   Your *chest* is the front of your body between your neck and your waist.

chestnut   A *chestnut* is the shiny brown nut of a *chestnut tree*.   You can play the game of conkers with *chestnuts*.

chew   To *chew* is to break up food in your mouth with your teeth before you swallow it.

chicken   A *chicken* is a young hen or a young cock.

child   A young boy or girl is a *child*. *Children* are older than babies and younger than adults.

chimney   Smoke from a fire goes up a *chimney* to the roof.   It is a long tube with bricks round it.

chin   Your *chin* is below your mouth and above your neck.

china   *China* is cups and saucers and plates made of a special clay.

chips   *Chips* are pieces of potato cut up and fried in fat or oil until they are brown and crisp.

Chips are small bits cut or broken off something.

chocolate   *Chocolate* is a hard, brown sweet made from cocoa and milk and sugar.   You can have a *chocolate* drink too.

choose   An apple, an orange, a banana, a pear, which will you *choose*? Which one will you pick? What will your *choice* be?

chop   To *chop* is to cut with a sharp blade, like vegetables on a *chopping board*.
Jack *chopped* down the beanstalk with an axe.

Christmas   *Christmas* is a happy time to remember the day Jesus *Christ* was born.   *Christmas Day* is on December 25 when people give presents and sing *Christmas carols* round the *Christmas tree*.

church   A *church* is a building where people pray.

cinema   A *cinema* is a place where you can see films.

circle   A *circle* is round like a ball or a ring or the letter O.

All the fun of the **circus** ring!

circus Acrobats and jugglers, animals and clowns all do clever things and funny tricks at the *circus*.

city A *city* is a very big and very busy town. London, New York and Tokyo are *cities*.

clap When you are happy or pleased you *clap* your hands. You bring your hands together and make a loud, sharp noise.

class A lot of pupils all together having lessons is a *class*. They learn in the *classroom*.

claw A *claw* is a hard nail on the foot of an animal or a bird. It is curved with a sharp tip. Crabs have two big *claws*.

clay *Clay* is a kind of soft earth that sticks together to make china and pots and bricks. The *clay* is baked to make it hard.

clean Your hands are *clean* after you wash them. They are not dirty.

clear When the sun shines in a *clear* blue sky, it is bright and open and without a cloud. When water is *clear* you can see right to the bottom.

clever   *Clever* is good at doing things or learning things or making things.
   The third Little Pig was *clever* to build his house of bricks.

cliff   A *cliff* is a very steep rocky hillside by the sea.

climb   To *climb is* to go up.
   Jack *climbed* the beanstalk.   He started at the bottom and went up higher and higher till he got to the top.

clock   A *clock* is a machine to tell you the time.

close   *Close* is very near. The house next door is *close* to your house.

close   (This *close* rhymes with rose.)
   To *close* is to shut.   When the door is *closed* it is not open.

cloth   Clothes are made of *cloth*. Bedclothes, tablecloths and bags are made of *cloth*.
   Cotton *cloth* is made from the cotton plant.
   Silkworms spin thread to make silk *cloth*.
   Woollen *cloth* comes from the sheep's thick coat.

clothes   All the things you wear are your *clothes*, from hat to shoes, from vest to jacket.

cloud   A *cloud* in the sky is made of lots and lots of little drops of water floating together.
   When the sky is *cloudy* you cannot see the sun.

clown   A *clown* is a funny man.   In a circus he paints his face and does funny things to make you laugh.

coach   Cinderella drove to the ball in a fine glass *coach* pulled by six horses.

   A *coach* is also a big bus that takes you on long journeys.

   Part of a railway train where the passengers sit is a *coach* too.

coal   *Coal* is black rock dug out of the ground.   It is burned to give heat.

coat   You wear a *coat* on top of all your other clothes to keep you warm on cold, windy days.

   A *coat* covers things like a *coat* of paint.

   A sheep's *coat* is its wool.

cock   A *cock* is a male bird.   A *cock* on the farm, cries 'Cock-a-doodle-doo' early in the morning.

cocoa   *Cocoa* comes from the beans of the cacao tree.   It is brown powder you make into a drink with water or milk.

coconut   A *coconut* is a big, hard hairy nut outside with white food and *coconut milk* inside.   It grows on the *coconut palm* tree.

coffee   *Coffee* is a drink made from the roasted beans of the *coffee tree*.

coin   A penny is a *coin*.   *Coins* are pieces of money made of metal.

cold   Ice is *cold*, snow is *cold*.   They are not hot.   If you are *cold* you shiver.

collar   The part of a coat, a shirt, a blouse or a dress that fits round your neck is a *collar*.

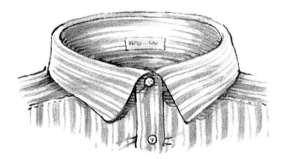

colour   Red is a *colour*, so is green and blue.   You will find lots of *colours* in this book.

comb   A *comb* is a piece of wood or metal or plastic with thin teeth.   You make your hair tidy or smooth when you *comb* it.

come   You move near when you *come* somewhere.   You arrive.
Red Riding Hood *came* at last to her grandmother's cottage.

comic   A funny person who makes you laugh is a *comic*.

A *comic* is also a paper or magazine full of funny pictures.

computer   A *computer* is a machine that stores away and gives the answers to things you want to know.

concert   You go to a *concert* to hear music and singing.

A **conductor** conducts the players at a **concert**.

conductor   Passengers buy a ticket for their journey from the *conductor* on a bus.

The *conductor* of an orchestra guides the players through the music.

cook   To *cook* is to roast or fry, boil or steam or bake food until it is ready to eat.   A *cook* heats food on a *cooker*.

cool   *Cool* is not hot and not cold, like a *cool* wind blowing.

copy   To *copy* is to do something or make something the same.
The teacher drew a cat on the blackboard and the children *copied* it in their drawing books.

corn   The seeds of plants like wheat and oats and barley and maize are called *corn*.

corner   The place where two streets meet or two walls meet is the *corner*.

cot   A little bed for a baby is a *cot*.

cottage   A *cottage* is a little house in the country.

cotton   The soft, white hairy part of the *cotton plant* makes *cotton* cloth for clothes and *cotton* thread for sewing.

couch   A *couch* is a long soft seat for two or three people to sit on.

count   *Count* the fingers on each hand. Add them up to see how many. You have *counted* from 1 to 10.

country   In the *country* are fields and woods and streams and farms.   It is the land outside towns and cities.

A *country* is also a part of the world where people live.   It is a land, like England, France or Australia.   They are all different *countries*.

cousin   Your *cousin* is the child of your aunt or uncle.

cover   To *cover* is to put one thing over another to hide it.   A tablecloth *covers* a table.   A cloud *covered* the sun.   The sun was hidden.

cow   A *cow* is a farm animal that gives milk.

cowboy   In America a *cowboy* looks after cows and bulls and calves on a large farm called a ranch.

How many **cows** did the **cowboy count**?

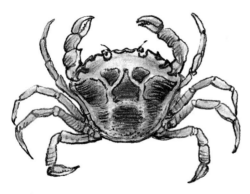

crab A *crab* is a sea animal with a hard shell, two big claws and eight legs.

crack A *crack* is a sharp noise like a nut being *cracked* with *nutcrackers*.

A *crack* is also a very thin opening like the *crack* in a *cracked* cup.

cradle A *cradle* is a little bed or cot for a baby.

crane A *crane* is a tall machine that lifts up big, heavy things.

crash A loud, breaking noise is a *crash*. Baby Bear's chair broke with a *crash* when Goldilocks sat on it.

crawl To *crawl* is to move about on hands and knees like a baby who cannot walk yet. Worms and snakes *crawl* by pulling their bodies along the ground.

crayon A *crayon* is a pencil or a stick of wax or chalk for making colour drawings.

cream The thick part at the top of milk is the *cream*.

crisp *Crisp* is dry and thin and easily broken, like *crisp* toast. *Crisps* are very thin slices of fried potato.

crocodile A *crocodile* is a large dangerous animal that lives in and near rivers in hot lands. It has a thick, bony skin, a long nose and huge jaws full of sharp teeth.

cross Anything shaped like + or × is a *cross*.

To *cross* is to go from one side to the other.

Cross also means angry.

crowd A *crowd* is a lot of people all together in one place. A *crowded* street is full of people.

crown A *crown* sits on the head of a king or a queen. It is made of gold and jewels.

crumb A *crumb* is a tiny piece of bread or cake.

The birds ate the *breadcrumbs* Hansel dropped.

crush To squeeze or press very hard is to *crush*.

crust   The hard or crisp outside of a loaf of bread is the *crust*.

cry   To give a loud shout is to *cry*.

To *cry* is also to be so sad or hurt that tears drop from your eyes.
The sad princess *cried* when her golden ball fell into the pool.

cup   A *cup* is a little bowl with a handle.   You drink a hot drink like tea and coffee from a *cup*.

cupboard   You can keep all sorts of things in a *cupboard*.   It has a door and shelves to hold anything from china to toys.

curl   A *curl* is a little ring or twist of hair.   *Curly* is not straight.
A pig has a *curly* tail.   It has a little curve in it.

curtain   A *curtain* hangs down by a window.   You can draw it across to cover the window at night and pull it open in the morning.

curve   A *curve* is a bend, like a bend in the road.   A *curve* is not a straight line.

cushion   A cloth bag full of feathers or air makes a soft *cushion* to sit on.

cut   You use a knife or scissors or a saw to *cut* things into smaller pieces.

How many **C** words can you find in the picture?

29

D d

daddy *Dad* and *daddy* are family names for father.

daffodil A *daffodil* is a bright yellow flower on a tall stalk, with a centre shaped like a trumpet. A *daffodil* grows from a bulb.

daily *Daily* is happening every day of the week, like sunrise and sunset.

daisy A *daisy* is a little wild flower with white, pink-tipped petals and a yellow centre.

dance At the ball the prince would *dance* only with Cinderella. They moved together in time to the music.

danger *Danger* is something that might hurt or harm you. It is *dangerous* to skate on thin ice. It is not safe.

dark *Dark* is not light. It is black as a night without moon or stars.

date The *date* is the day of the month and the year. A calendar shows you what *date* it is.

A *date* is also the shiny, brown fruit of a palm tree.

daughter A *daughter* is a girl child in a family.

dawn *Dawn* is sunrise when the first light of morning is in the sky.

day One *day* lasts for twenty-four hours. *Daytime* is the time between sunrise and sunset when there is *daylight* in the sky.

dead *Dead* is not living or alive any more, like *dead* leaves that fall from the trees.

dear *Dear* is very much loved, like a *dear* child or a *dear* friend.

If you buy something *dear*, you spend a lot of money. It is not cheap.

December *December* is the twelfth and last month of the year. It has 31 days. Christmas is in *December*.

deck The floor on a ship or a boat is the *deck*.

decorate To *decorate* is to add pretty things to make something more beautiful.

A Christmas tree is *decorated* with coloured balls and little lights and other *decorations*.

To *decorate* a room is to give it a new coat of paint or paper.

Two **deer** drink at a **deep** pool.

deep   The princess's golden ball fell into a *deep* pool.   It was too far down for her to reach it.

deer   A *deer* is a wild animal that runs very fast on long thin legs.   A male *deer* has horns called antlers growing like branches from its head.

den   A *den* is the home some wild animals make for themselves. Lions and foxes live in *dens*.

dentist   A *dentist* looks after people's teeth.

desert   *Desert* is dry, sandy land where there is little water and few things grow.

desk   A *desk* is a table where you can write and read.   Some *desks* have drawers.

diamond   A *diamond* is a very hard precious stone.   When cut and polished, *diamonds* are bright jewels.

diary   A *diary* is a book for writing down what happens every day.

dictionary   A book of words from A to Z is a *dictionary*.   It tells you what the words mean.

die   To *die* is to stop living.

different   The Three Little Pigs built *different* kinds of houses.   They were not the same at all.

31

difficult   *Difficult* is not easy.   A *difficult* job is hard to do.

dig   You turn over the earth with a spade when you *dig*.   You take out earth when you *dig* a hole.
   The Seven Dwarfs *dug* gold out of the mountain.

dinner   *Dinner* is the biggest meal of the day.

dinosaur   A *dinosaur* was an animal with skin like a crocodile that lived on Earth a very long time ago. Some *dinosaurs* were huge and some were very small.

dirty   *Dirty* is not clean.   *Dirty* is covered in *dirt* and needing to be washed.

disappear   To go out of sight or vanish is to *disappear*.

disc   A *disc* is flat and round like a flat plate.

   A *disc* is also a record.   A *disc jockey* plays records on a record player.   People dance to records at a *disco*.

dish   A *dish* is a shallow bowl for food. *Dishes* are all the things you use for eating and drinking, like cups and saucers and plates.

dive   To go down head first into water is to *dive*.   An aeroplane *dives* nose first and very fast through the air.
   The Frog Prince *dived* into the pool to fetch the princess's golden ball.

diver   A *diver* works underwater in a special *diving suit*.

doctor   A *doctor* takes care of you when you are sick.

dog   A *dog* is a four-legged animal, large or small, smooth-haired or curly-haired.   *Dogs* are good pets and some *dogs* are good workers.

doll   A *doll* is a small toy person for children to play with.

donkey   A *donkey* is a tame animal that looks like a horse but has long ears.
   A *donkey* is also called an ass.

door   A *door* is the way in and the way out of a house or a room or a building.
   Doors open and shut.

double   *Double* is two times or twice as big or twice as much.   *Double* 3 is 6.

down   The wolf came *down* the Little Pig's chimney.   He fell from the top to the bottom.
  When you come *downstairs* from upstairs you come *down* to the floor below.

dragon   A *dragon* is a fearsome animal you meet in storybooks.   It has horny skin and wings and breathes out fire.

draw   You make a picture when you *draw* with pencils or crayons or chalks.   You have *drawn* a *drawing*.

Draw also means to pull.
  Cinderella's glass coach was *drawn* by six white horses.

drawer   A *drawer* is a box to keep things in, inside a piece of furniture. *Drawers* slide in and out of tables or chests or desks.

dream   In a *dream* you see pictures and have thoughts while you sleep.

Have you ever seen a **dragon** in your **dreams**?

33

dress You put on your clothes when you *dress*.
     A girl or a woman wears a *dress*.   The top and the skirt of a *dress* are in one piece.

drink You swallow liquid when you *drink*.

drive To *drive* is to make a machine move and work.   You can go for a *drive* in a car.
     Cinderella *drove* in a glass coach.

A *drive* can also be the path to a house.

drop You let something fall when you *drop* it.
     Hansel *dropped* white pebbles on the ground to show the way home.

A *drop* is also a little bubble of liquid, like a *raindrop*.

drum A *drum* is a round musical instrument with a skin stretched tight across the top.   A *drummer* beats a *drum* with *drumsticks*.

dry *Dry* is not wet.   After bathing you *dry* yourself with a towel.

duck A *duck* is a bird that can swim as well as fly.   Its beak is flat and it makes a sound like 'quack'.

dust Tiny bits of dirt flying in the air float down to cover things in *dust*.

A *dustbin* is a big metal or plastic can to hold dirt and rubbish.

A *duster* is a cloth to wipe away *dust*.

dwarf A *dwarf* is a very little person.
     Snow White looked after seven little *dwarfs* and they looked after her.

Seven little **drummer dwarfs** make a lot of noise.

E e

each   *Each* is every one.   *Each* week has 7 days.

ear   You have an *ear* on each side of your head.   *Ears* are for hearing.

Earrings are rings or jewels to decorate ears.

early   *Early* is not late.   *Early* is in good time.   *Early* is also before the time fixed.
   The Little Pig got to the apple orchard *early*.   He was there before the wolf.   He was *earlier* than the wolf.

earth   The *Earth* is our world where we live.

Earth is also the ground where things grow.

east   The *east* is where the sun rises. The *east* is opposite to the west.

Easter   *Easter* is a holiday to mark Jesus's rise from the dead.

easy   *Easy* is not hard or difficult.   You can do *easy* jobs *easily*, without any trouble at all.

eat   To *eat* is to put food in your mouth, taste it, chew it and swallow it.

edge   The *edge* is the very end or the rim.   It is where a thing stops.

The *edge* is also the sharp cutting part of a knife.

egg   Birds, fish and insects lay *eggs*. Some baby animals like chickens live inside the *eggshell* until they are born.

eight   *Eight* is 8.   It is one more than 7.   *Eighteen* is 18.   Ten and *eight* make *eighteen*.   *Eighty* is 80. *Eighty* is ten times *eight*.

Eight coloured **eggs** are ready for **Easter**.

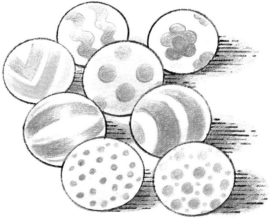

elbow   Your *elbow* is the joint in the middle of your arm.   Your arm bends at the *elbow*.

electricity   *Electricity* makes light and heat and makes machines go.

Eleven large elephants show off their long trunks.

elephant   An *elephant* is the biggest animal that lives on land.   It has a long nose called a trunk, two long sharp teeth called tusks and big floppy ears.

eleven   *Eleven* is 11.   It is one more than ten.   Some sports teams have *eleven* players.

empty   An *empty* box has nothing in it.   There is nobody living in an *empty* house.
   If you *empty* a room you take everything out.

end   The *end* is where something finishes or stops.   Z is at the *end* of the alphabet.
   Dick Whittington's journey *ended* in London.
   Most fairy stories have a happy *ending*.

enemy   An *enemy* is not your friend. An *enemy* fights against you.
   The wicked queen was Snow White's *enemy*.

engine   A machine that makes things go or work is an *engine*, like a *steam engine*, a *petrol engine* or a *railway engine*.

enjoy   To *enjoy* is to have a happy time doing things you like to do.

enough   *Enough* is just as much as you need.   It is not too much and not too little.

envelope   You put a letter or a packet in an *envelope*.   It is a paper bag, thin or thick, little or big, to fold over, stick down and put in the post.

escape Hansel and Gretel at last made their *escape* from the witch's cottage.   They ran away and were free.   They *escaped*.

even *Even* is flat and smooth, with no bumps.

evening *Evening* comes at the end of the day and just before night falls.

ever *Ever* is always.
   Every is each one or all. Christmas comes round *every* December.
   Everybody or *everyone* are all the people.
   Everywhere is here and there and all over the place.

excited You have a happy feeling before you do something nice or new or different.   You are *excited*.
   An *exciting* story is full of thrills and adventure.

exercise To *exercise* is to bend and stretch, walk and run, to help you keep fit.

eye You have an *eye* on each side of your nose.   *Eyes* are for seeing.
   An *eyebrow* is a line of hairs above each *eye*.
   Eyelashes are hairs growing along the edge of each *eyelid*.
   An *eyelid* is a little cover over each *eye*.   *Eyelids* open and shut when you are awake, and stay shut when you are asleep.

F f

face   Your *face* is the front part of your head from forehead to chin.

factory   A *factory* is a building where things are made, usually with machines.   All kinds of things from cars to carpets are made in *factories*.

fair   *Fair* is light in colour like *fair* hair.

Fair is fine like the weather on a sunny day.

A *fair* is a place for fun, with rides and roundabouts and games with prizes.

fairy   A *fairy* is a small, magical person with wings you meet in *fairy* stories.

fall   To tumble or drop or come down is to *fall*.

The wolf *fell* down the Little Pig's chimney.

family   A mother, a father and their child or their children make a *family*.

famous   *Famous* means well known to lots of people, like a *famous* singer or a *famous* footballer.

far   *Far* is not near.   *Far* is a long way away.

farm   Animals are kept on a *farm*. Corn and other foods are grown on a *farm*.   The *farmer* looks after them all.

fast *Fast* is very quick.

Fast is fixed or stuck very hard.

fasten To *fasten* is to close or to lock. To *fasten* is to join or tie together like the two ends of a seatbelt.

fat *Fat* is big, wide, round, heavy.

father A *father* is a man with a child or children of his own.

favourite Which fairy story is your *favourite*? Your *favourite* is the one you like best.

fear Lost in the wood, Hansel and Gretel could not help being full of *fear*. They were afraid.
Fearless is brave.
Fearsome is frightening and terrible.

feather A soft, light piece from a bird's coat is a *feather*. Birds' *feathers* help them to fly and to keep warm.

February *February* is the second month of the year. It has 28 days and 29 days in a leap year. A leap year happens every four years.

feed You give food to people when you *feed* them. Plants and animals are *fed* too.

feel To *feel* is to touch. The point of a pin *feels* sharp when you touch it.

You *feel* hot in the sun. Your body tells you it is hot.

Cinderella *felt* happy at the ball. She knew she was glad.

female A *female* is a girl or a woman.

A cow is a *female* animal.

fence A *fence* is put round a garden or a field to close it in. *Fences* are made of wood or wooden posts with wire between.

ferry A *ferry* is a boat to carry people and cars across water.

fetch To *fetch* is to carry or to bring.
'*Fetch* me my magic hen,' roared the giant to his wife.

few *Few* is not many or hardly any at all.

field A piece of land where grass grows, or corn or vegetables grow is a *field*.

A *field* is also smooth grass where ball games are played.

fight A *fight* is a battle between enemies.
A *fight* can be a boxing match.
To *fight* is to strike with fists or with weapons.

fill To leave no more room is to *fill*. To make quite full, like a glass *filled* to the top.

film   A *film* is a moving picture show at the cinema or on television.   You put a *film* in a camera to take photographs.

find   To see something you have lost is to *find* it.   To see something just by chance is also to *find* it.

fine   On a *fine* day the weather is sunny and fair.

Fine is very good.

Fine is also very thin, like thread or *fine* hair.

A *fine* is money to pay for doing something wrong.

finger   A *finger* is part of your hand.   One hand has five *fingers*, two hands have ten *fingers*.

finish   To *finish* is to come to an end, or get to the end.   To *finish* is to stop.   Goldilocks *finished* Baby Bear's porridge.

fire   A *fire* is something burning.   Hot flames and smoke rise from a *fire*.   A *fire engine* quickly carries *firemen* and ladders and hoses to put out *fires*.

fireworks   *Fireworks* are lit for fun. They are pretty showers of coloured lights and often go off with a bang.

first   *First* is at the beginning.   *First* is before or better or quicker than all the others.   Number 1 is the *first* number.

fish   A *fish* is a swimming animal that lives only in water.
To *fish* is to catch *fish* with a rod or a net.   *Fishermen* in *fishing boats* catch *fish* in big nets.

fist   Your hand is a *fist* when you curl and close your fingers tightly.
Boxers fight with their *fists*.

fit   To *fit* is to be just the right size.
The glass slipper *fitted* only Cinderella's foot.

Fit is also well and healthy.

five   *Five* is 5.   It is one more than four.   Your hand has *five* fingers.   *Fifteen* is 15.   Ten and *five* are *fifteen*.   *Fifty* is 50.   *Fifty* is ten times *five*.

fix   To *fix* is to mend or put right something that does not work or is broken.

flag   A *flag* is a piece of cloth with a special pattern like a cross or stars or stripes.   Every country has a *flag* of its own.   A *flag* often hangs from a *flagpole* or a ship's mast.

flame   A *flame* is a bright, burning burst of fire.

flat   *Flat* is smooth and even.   When you lie *flat* you stretch out in one straight line.

In a big building, a *flat* is a set of rooms to live in.

flavour   Everything you eat and drink has its own *flavour*.   It is its special taste.

float   Things that *float*, sit or move on top of the water.   They do not sink.

flood   In a *flood* too much water in a river or a lake flows out over the land.

floor   The *floor* of a room is under your feet.   You stand and walk and dance on the *floor*.

flour   *Flour* is fine powder made from wheat and used in baking.

flow   To *flow* is to run like water in a river or out of a tap.

flower   A *flower* is the beautiful head of a plant.

fly   To *fly* is to move through the air like a bird or an aeroplane.
A *fly* is a little insect with wings.

fog   *Fog* is a cloud of thick wet mist.   It is not easy to see things on a *foggy* day.

fold   To *fold* is to bend or double something over.

follow   To come behind or go after is to *follow*.   Tuesday *follows* Monday. The Frog Prince *followed* the princess home to the palace.

food   Everything we eat to keep us alive is *food*.

foot   Your *foot* is at the end of your leg.   You stand and walk and run on your two *feet*.

football   A *football* is a ball players kick in a game of *football*.

forehead   Between your hair and your eyes is your *forehead*.

forest   A *forest* is a very big wood full of trees.

forget   When you *forget* something you do not remember.   It slips from your mind.

fork   A *fork* is for picking up food from your plate.   A *garden fork* is a tool for digging and lifting.

four   *Four* is 4.   It is one more than three.   *Fourteen* is 14.   Ten and *four* make *fourteen*.   *Forty* is 40.   *Forty* is ten times *four*.

fox   A *fox* is a wild animal that looks like a dog with pointed ears and a bushy tail.

free   *Free* is for nothing.   *Free* is paying no money.

To be *free* also means you can do what you want or go where you like.   You are not a prisoner.

freeze   To *freeze* is to turn liquid to ice.   It was so cold the pond *froze* over.

A *freezer* or *deepfreeze freezes* food and keeps it fresh.

fresh *Fresh* is new and good like *freshly* baked bread.

Fresh is also cold and clean like a *fresh* wind.

Friday *Friday* is the sixth day of the week.

friend A *friend* is someone you like very much and who likes you too.

fright Goldilocks got a *fright* when she woke to see the Three Bears.   She was suddenly very *frightened* and afraid.

frog A *frog* is a small animal that lives in or near water.   It has long back legs for hopping.

from *From* is not to.   *From* is away from and not towards.
From is out of.   Cheese is made *from* milk.

front The *front* is the face of anything. Your face is at the *front* of your head.
In front is before and not behind.

frost *Frost* is a white icy cover on grass and trees and roofs and roads when the weather is very cold.

fruit Cherries are the *fruit* of the cherry tree, raspberries are the *fruit* of a raspberry bush.
The *fruit* is the part of a tree or a plant that holds the seeds.

fry To *fry* is to cook with hot fat or oil in a *frying pan*.

full *Full* is filled to the top.   *Full* is packed, like a bus with every seat taken.
Red Riding Hood carried a basket *full* of good things.

fun *Fun* is happiness and joy.   *Fun* is enjoying yourself.
Funny things make you laugh, like jokes and comics and *funny* films.

fur *Fur* is the thick, soft hairy coat of some animals.   Cats are *furry*.

furniture Chairs and tables and chests and beds are useful pieces of *furniture* in a room.

Three **furry** cats fast aleep on the **furniture**.

43

G g

game   A *game* is played for fun, inside, like *card games* and *party games*, or outside, like *ball games* and *chasing games*.

garage
Cars are kept in a *garage*.   Cars are mended and filled with petrol in a *garage*.

garden   A *garden* is a piece of ground, big or small, where flowers and trees and fruit and vegetables grow.

gate   A *gate* is a doorway in a wall or a fence or a hedge.

gather   To *gather* is to put things together like a bunch of flowers.
   To *gather* is to come together like a crowd of people or clouds before a storm.

gentle   *Gentle* is soft and light, like a *gentle* wind.   *Gentle* is quiet and kind and not rough and wild.

giant   A *giant* is a huge person or a huge thing.   In fairy stories a *giant* is very big, very strong and very fearsome.

giraffe   A *giraffe* is the tallest animal on Earth. It has very long legs and a very long neck.

girl   A *girl* is a child who will be a woman when she is older.

give   To *give* is to hand over, like a present.
   Jack *gave* his mother the giant's magic hen.

glad   *Glad* is pleased and happy and full of joy.

glass   *Glass* is hard and can be so clear you can see right through it. Windows and drinking *glasses* and bottles are made of *glass*.

A *glass* is also a *looking glass* or a mirror.

Glasses help people to see better by making things look clearer or bigger.

Glasses help him see himself in the **looking-glass**.

glide   To *glide* is to slide smoothly over water or through the air.
A *glider* is an aeroplane without an engine that *glides* with the wind.

glove   A *glove* covers your hand. *Gloves* have spaces for every finger.

glue   *Glue* sticks things together.

go   To *go* is to move from one place to another.   To *go* is to take a journey.
'You will *go* to the ball,' said Cinderella's fairy godmother.   And she *went* to the ball.

goat   A *goat* is an animal like a sheep but it has pointed horns and a beard.   *Goats* give milk.

gold   The giant's money bags were full of *gold* coins.   They were made of bright yellow precious metal.

goldfish   A *goldfish* is a little golden-red fish often kept in a tank as a pet.

good   *Good* is nice and kind and polite and clever.   *Good* things please and make you happy.

goodbye   You say '*Goodbye*' when you go away.

goose   A *goose* is a bird that can swim and fly and lay eggs.   *Geese* are bigger than ducks and have long necks.

grand   *Grand* is large and great and rich and wonderful.

grandfather   A *grandfather* is the father of a father or a mother.

grandmother   A *grandmother* is the mother of a mother or a father.

How many **grandfathers** and **grandmothers** will there be in the photograph?

grape A *grape* is a little fruit, green or red or purple that grows in bunches on a vine.

grass *Grass* is the thin green leaves growing thickly in fields and on lawns and hillsides.

great *Great* is very big and grand and wonderful.

greedy A *greedy* person wants more than he needs, takes more than he needs, eats more than he needs.

green *Green* is the colour of spring and summer leaves. *Green* is the colour of grass and lettuce and *green* beans. A *greengrocer* sells all kinds of vegetables and fruit.

grey *Grey* is the colour of the sky when it rains. *Grey* is the colour of an elephant's skin.

Green grass with **grey** elephant.

grill To *grill* is to cook under a *grill* on a cooker or over a fire.
   A *grill* on the cooker heats meat from above.
   A barbecue *grill* has bars to put meat on.

grocer A *grocer* sells all sorts of foods, from coffee to cheese, from biscuits to bacon.

ground We stand and walk on the *ground*. Plants and trees grow out of the *ground*. The *ground* is the earth.

grow To *grow* is to get bigger. Babies *grow* into boys and girls.
   Jack's beans *grew* into a very big beanstalk.

growl Angry animals *growl*. They make a low, cross noise in their throats.

guess If you do not know the answer you can *guess* it. You might be right or you might be wrong.

guide Hansel knew the white pebbles would *guide* them home. They would show the way. They would lead them home.

guitar A *guitar* is a musical instrument with strings to pluck with your fingers.

gun A *gun* is a weapon that shoots bullets. Big *guns* shoot shells.

gymnasium A *gymnasium* is a place to do exercises. It is full of things to help you keep fit.

H h

hair Black or brown, fair or red, long or short, straight or curly, *hair* grows on heads and on men's faces.
A *hairbrush* keeps it tidy.
A *hairdresser* cuts, washes and shapes it.
A coconut has a *hairy* skin.

half If you cut a cake through the middle you have two pieces the same size. Each piece is a *half*. Two *halves* make a whole. *Half* is ½.

ham *Ham* is meat from a pig's leg. It is usually salt or smoked.

hamburger A round flat cake of meat chopped very small and fried or grilled is a *hamburger*.

hammer A *hammer* is a tool with a handle and a heavy head. You knock in nails with a *hammer*.

hand Your *hand* is at the end of your arm. *Hands* are *handy* for holding things.

handbag A *handbag* is a light little bag to carry things by hand.

handkerchief A *handkerchief* is a soft piece of cloth or paper for wiping or blowing your nose.

handle A cup, a jug, a pot, a bucket, a basket all have a *handle* to hold them by.

hang Pictures *hang* from hooks, washing *hangs* from a clothes line. They are fixed at the top and free at the bottom.
The princess's long, long hair *hung* nearly to the ground.

happen To *happen* is to take place. What *happened* when Jack's mother threw away the beans?

happy *Happy* is glad and full of joy. Snow White and her prince lived *happily* ever after. They were full of *happiness*.

harbour A *harbour* is a safe place for ships to stay.

hard *Hard* is not soft. *Hard* is tough and stony like rocks.
Hard is not easy, *hard* is difficult.

Hold a **hammer** in your **hand** to knock in a nail.

47

hare A *hare* is an animal like a big rabbit with longer ears and longer legs.

harm To *harm* is to hurt or give pain.

hat You wear a *hat* on your head. It covers your head and keeps it warm.

hay *Hay* is cut and dried grass to feed horses and cows.
  Tom Thumb fell asleep in the *hay* and was swallowed by a cow.

head Your *head* is at the top of your body above your neck.

  Head is also first and highest, or most important like a *headteacher*.

health *Health* is how your body feels. In good *health* you are fit and well and happy and *healthy*.

heap A *heap* is a pile of things gathered together.

hear Listen with your ears and you will *hear* all sorts of sounds.
  Cinderella *heard* the clock strike twelve.

heart Inside your body the *heart* pumps blood to every part of you.

heat *Heat* is warmth like the hot rays from the sun.
  To *heat* is to make things hot.

heavy A heavy *load* is hard to lift or carry. It is of great weight.

hedge A *hedge* is a row of bushes growing thick and close together. A *hedge* makes a fence round a field or a garden.

hedgehog A *hedgehog* is a little animal with a prickly back.

A **hedgehog** crawls out of a **hedge**.

heel   Your *heel* is the back of your foot.   The *heel* of a shoe fits round your *heel*.

height   Your *height* is how tall you are.   The *height* of a hill is how *high* it is.

helicopter   A *helicopter* is an aeroplane with no wings.   It is lifted straight up into the air and flies with great whirling blades.

help   You make someone's job easier to do when you *help*.   You are being *helpful*.

hen   A *hen* is a female bird that lays eggs.

here   *Here* is not there.   *Here* is where you are at this minute.

hero   A *hero* is a very brave or wonderful man or boy.   A very brave or wonderful woman or girl is a *heroine*.

hide   No one can see you when you *hide*.   If you *hide* a thing you put it out of sight.
   Jack *hid* in the oven out of sight of the giant.   He was *hidden*.

high   *High* is tall.
   Jack's beanstalk grew *high* into the sky.   No one knows what *height* it was.

hill   A *hill* is high ground.   Climb a *hillside* to the top and you are high above the ground.

hippopotamus   A *hippopotamus* is a huge animal with short legs living in the rivers in hot lands.

49

hit To *hit* is to strike or to knock. Balls are *hit* with bats. Nails are *hit* with hammers.

hobby A *hobby* is something you like to do in your spare time.

hold Boxes and barrels and bins and baskets *hold* things. They can all have things in them. Your hands *hold* things too.
  The Three Bears' bowls *held* porridge.

hole A *hole* is an opening in anything at all, from a *hole* in your sock to a *mousehole* in the wall.

holiday No school! No work! It's fun and play at *holiday* time.

holly *Holly* is a tree with dark green, shiny leaves all year round and bright red berries in winter.

home *Home* is where you live. *Home* can be a cottage or a castle, a flat or a farmhouse.

honey *Honey* is sweet and yellow and made by bees from the nectar of flowers.

hook A *hook* is a bent piece of metal to catch things, like a *fish hook*, or to hang things, like a *picture hook*.
  Hooked is bent or curved like a parrot's beak.

hope To *hope* is to wish something you want will come true.

horn A *horn* is a bone growing on some animals' heads. A male deer has *horns* called antlers.
  Horny is bony and hard.

A *horn* is a musical instrument you blow to make music.

horrible   *Horrible* is terrible and nasty and not nice at all.

horse   A *horse* is a fine animal to ride. A *horse* is a useful animal to pull wagons and coaches.

hose   A *hose* is a long tube to carry water from a tap.
   A gardener waters a garden with a *hose*.   Firemen put out fires with *hoses*.

hospital   Sick people are looked after in *hospital* by doctors and nurses.

hot   *Hot* is very warm like a *hot* drink of cocoa or like you on a warm, sunny day.

hotel   A *hotel* is a place you pay to stay in and sleep in and eat in.

hour   The time between 1 o'clock and 2 o'clock is one *hour*.   An *hour* is 60 minutes.   A day has 24 *hours*.

house   A *house* is a building to live in.   A *house* is a home.

hovercraft   A *hovercraft* carries you over water and land on a cushion of air.

hug   To give someone a *hug* you put your arms right round him and hold him tight.

huge   *Huge* is very, very big like a giant or an elephant or a whale.

Look out little mouse!
Huge feet are near.

hum   A *hum* is a long low sound like m-m-m-m-m-m.
   You *hum* when you sing with your lips closed.

hump   A *hump* is a round bump on a camel's back.

51

hundred A *hundred* is 100. A *hundred* is ten times ten.

A **hundred** little faces are smiling out at you.

hungry You want to eat when you are *hungry*. You need food.

hurry You move fast when you *hurry*. Cinderella *hurried* from the palace when the clock struck twelve.

hurt To *hurt* is to give pain. Even under ten mattresses the little hard pea *hurt* the real princess.

husband A *husband* is a man who is married. When Cinderella married her prince, he became her *husband*.

hydrofoil A *hydrofoil* is a fast light boat that slides over water on blades like skis.

I i

ice   *Ice* is water frozen hard by the cold.

ice cream   *Ice cream* is a cold sweet food made from cream and sugar frozen together.

ill   *Ill* is sick and not feeling well.

important   *Important* is valuable. *Important* things must be done. They come first.
   Important people are special and clever.   They are not ordinary.

insect   An *insect* is a very small animal with six legs.   Wasps and bees and ants and flies are *insects*.

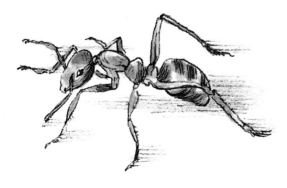

inside   When you are *inside* you are not outside.
   Jack hid *inside* the oven.

instead   *Instead* means in place of something else or somebody else.
   Instead of rags Cinderella wore a beautiful dress.

instrument   An *instrument* is a special tool made to do a special job.

   A *musical instrument* is made to play music.

inventor   An *inventor* makes or thinks of something new.

invite   When you *invite* friends to tea you ask them to come.
   The wicked witch *invited* Hansel and Gretel into her cottage made of sweets and cake.

iron   *Iron* is a hard, heavy, grey metal.

   An *iron* is a tool you heat up to smooth and press clothes.

island   Land with water all round it is an *island*.

J j

jacket A *jacket* is a short coat.

jam *Jam* is fruit and sugar boiled together until it is thick.

January *January* is the first month of the year. It has 31 days.

jar A *jar* holds all kinds of things. It has a wide top, often has a lid and is made of glass or baked clay.

jaw Your *jaw* is the bone in your mouth that holds your teeth.

jeans *Jeans* are trousers made of thick, strong cotton.

jelly Fruit juice and sugar boiled together make *jelly*.

Jelly is also a clear sweet pudding.

jet plane A *jet plane* is an aeroplane that flies very fast through the air.

jewel A *jewel* is a precious stone. A diamond is a *jewel*.

Jewellery is necklaces and rings and bracelets made of jewels and often gold or silver.

jigsaw Pieces of a picture fit together to make a *jigsaw puzzle*.

job A *job* is work. A *job* is something to work at.

jog To *jog* is to run slowly for exercise.

join To *join* is to stick or tie or fasten two things together.

joint A *joint* is the place where two things are *joined* together, like the bones in your body.

joke A *joke* is a funny thing or a funny story to make you laugh.

jolly *Jolly* is happy and bright and full of fun.

journey You make a *journey* when you travel from one place to another.

joy The prince was full of *joy* to find Cinderella. He felt great happiness.

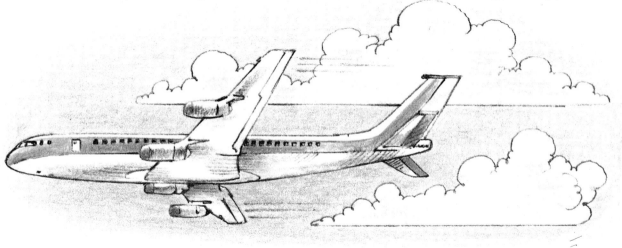

A **juggler** juggling **jugs** spills **juice** on his **jumper**.

jug   A *jug* holds water and milk and lots of other liquids.   A *jug* has a handle and a little lip to pour from.

juggler   A *juggler* tosses and catches lots of things at once and never lets them fall.

juice   *Juice* is the liquid inside fruit and vegetables.   Squeeze a *juicy* orange and you'll have *orange juice*.

July   *July* is the seventh month of the year.   It has 31 days.

jump   To *jump* is to spring up or down or over with both feet off the ground.

jumper   Pull a warm, woolly *jumper* over your head to cover the top half of your body.
   A *jumper* is also called a pullover, a sweater or a jersey.

June   *June* is the sixth month of the year.   It has 30 days.

jungle   In hot lands, the *jungle* is a thick, dark, forest of trees and bushes and grasses.   The *jungle* is the home of many wild animals.

just   *Just* is a moment ago or the moment before.
   Jack had *just* picked up the magic hen when the giant woke up.

K k

kangaroo   A *kangaroo* is an animal with big strong legs to jump with, a long thick tail and a pocket in front to carry its babies.

keep   To *keep* is to have or hold on to things for yourself.
  You *keep* smaller things in bigger things like books in a bookcase or socks in a drawer.   They are *kept* there.

kettle   You boil water in a *kettle*.   It is made of metal and has a handle and a spout to pour from.

key   A *key* is a piece of metal to fit into a lock.   Turn the *key* one way to open a door and the other way to lock it.

  A piano has *keys* for the fingers to play.   A computer has *keys* for the fingers to tap.

kick   To *kick* is to hit with your foot.

kind   *Kind* is good and friendly and helpful and nice.

  Kind also means sort.   What *kind* of stories do you like best?

king   A *king* rules a country.   He is his country's head man.

kiss   To *kiss* is to touch with your lips someone you like.
  The princess *kissed* the frog and he turned into a prince.

kitchen   A *kitchen* is the room where the cooking is done.

kite   A *kite* is a flying toy made of paper or cloth fastened to strips of light wood.

Up and away go **kitten** and **kite**.

kitten   A *kitten* is a baby cat.

knee   Your *knee* is the joint in the middle of your leg where it bends.

kneel   You rest on your knee or your knees when you *kneel*.
  The prince *knelt* to kiss Sleeping Beauty.

knife   A *knife* is for cutting.   It is a sharp metal blade with a handle.

knit   To *knit* is to make balls of wool into clothes with *knitting needles*.

knob   A *knob* is a little handle to open a door or drawer.

knock   When you *knock* at a door you give quick sharp blows with your knuckles.   When you *knock* other things you hit or bump into them very hard.

knot   String or rope or laces or ribbon are tied together with a *knot*.

know   If you *know* a thing you are sure it is true.
   If you *know* a person you have met him before.
   Knowledge is things that are *known*.

knuckle   A *knuckle* is a joint in your finger.   You can knock on doors with your *knuckles*.

If the door **knob** won't turn, **knock** with your **knuckles**.

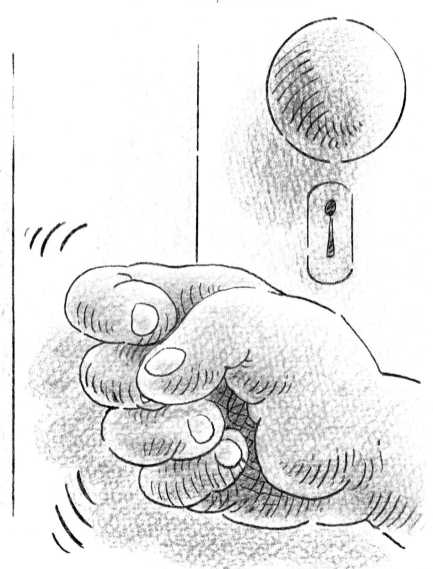

L l

lace To *lace* is to pull a string through little holes in your shoe and tie it with a bow.

Lace is fine cloth made with a pretty pattern of holes.

ladder Two long poles with steps between make a *ladder* to climb up to high places.

lady A *lady* is another name for a woman.

A **lady** on a **ladder**.

lake A *lake* is a large piece of water with land all round it.

lamb A *lamb* is a baby sheep.

lamp A *lamp* is lit to give brightness. The *lamp* on a tall *lamp post* lights up a dark street.

land *Land* is the earth or the ground where we live. There is no water on land.

Aeroplanes come down to earth when they *land*.

large *Large* is very big, like an elephant, a whale or a giant.

last *Last* is not first. *Last* is at the end and after everything else.

To *last* is to go on for a time. Sleeping Beauty's sleep *lasted* for a hundred years.

late *Late* is not early. *Late* is after the right time. If a train is *late* it will not arrive on time. It arrives *later* than it should. The *latest* news is the newest news.

laugh   A *laugh* is a jolly sound to make when you are happy or something is funny.

Everyone *laughed* at the emperor's new clothes.   The street was full of *laughter*.

launderette   We get clothes washed and dried in washing machines at a *launderette* or a *laundromat*.

law   A *law* is a rule you must obey.

lawn   A *lawn* is short, smooth grass in a garden.   A *lawn* is cut short with a *lawn mower*.

lay   To *lay* is to put down like your head on the pillow.

To *lay* a table you put down knives and forks and spoons and plates, and the table is *laid*.

Hens give eggs when they *lay*.

lazy   *Lazy* people like to do nothing. They do not want to work.

lead   To *lead* is to go in front to show the way.   To *lead* is to guide.

Hansel's white pebbles *led* Hansel and Gretel home.

leaf   A *leaf* is flat and green and grows on a tree or a plant.   All *leaves* have different shapes.

lean   You do not stand up straight when you *lean*.   You rest against something like a ladder against a wall.

Lean people are thin people.   *Lean* meat is not fat meat.

leap   To *leap* is to jump high or jump far.

learn   To *learn* is to find out.   To *learn* is to get to know things or how to do things.

leather   *Leather* is made from the skins of some animals and used for lots of things like bags and shoes and gloves and jackets.

leave   You go away when you *leave*. Cinderella *left* the ball at midnight.

If you *leave* a thing, you do not take it with you.

left   You have a *left* hand and a right hand.   Your *left* is on the opposite side to your right.

leg   At the bottom of your body you have two *legs* to stand and walk and run on.

lemon   A *lemon* is a bright yellow fruit full of sour tasting juice.   Add sugar and water to *lemon juice* for a drink of fresh *lemonade*.

lend   You let someone have something of yours for a time when you *lend*. You get back what you *lend*. A library *lends* you books. You get them on *loan*.

length   How long a thing is from one end to the other is its *length*.

less   *Less* is not so much.
There was *less* porridge in Baby Bear's bowl than in Daddy Bear's and Mummy Bear's.

let   '*Let* me in, Little Pig,' said the wicked wolf.   'Allow me to come into your house.'
But the Little Pig did not *let* him.

letter   A *letter* is writing on paper.   Put it in an envelope and post it.

A *letter* of the alphabet is any one from A to Z.

lettuce   A *lettuce* is a plant with big green leaves, good to eat raw in a fresh green salad.

library   Shelves full of books to read make a *library*.   A big building full of books to borrow is a *library*.

lick   To *lick* is to taste and eat with your tongue, like ice cream and lollipops.

lid   A *lid* is a top or a cover.   *Lids* come off or open and shut.
Boxes have *lids*, pots and pans have *lids*.
Your eyes have *eyelids*.

lie   You *lie* when you rest in bed.   Your body is flat.   You are not standing, you are *lying*.
Hansel and Gretel *lay* asleep under the trees.

To *lie* is to say something not true.

life   *Life* is being alive.   *Life* is living.

lift   To *lift* is to pick up.   To *lift* is to move to a higher place.
The prince *lifted* Snow White onto his horse.

light   *Light* is brightness, like *sunlight* or *moonlight* or *firelight* or *electric light*.

Light is not heavy.   *Light* is easy to carry or easy to lift.

lighthouse   Tall like a tower, with a strong light at the top, a *lighthouse* stands in or near the sea to warn sailors of hidden dangers.

lightning   In a thunderstorm, *lightning* is a flash of brightness that lights up the sky.

Lightning and **lighthouse light** up the sky.

like To *like* is to enjoy and think something is good.   To *like* is to think someone is nice.

Like means nearly the same.   The sound of a drum is *like* thunder.

line A *line* is a thin mark like a pencil mark.   A *line* can be straight or curved.

A *line* is any long thin thing, like a *clothes line* or a *fishing line*.

When you stand *in line* you are in a long, straight row of people.

lion A *lion* is a wild animal that lives in hot lands.   It is like a very big cat with a yellow-brown coat and a lot of thick hair, called a mane, on its neck and head.

A *lioness* is a female *lion* and has no mane.

lip You have a top *lip* and a bottom *lip* round your mouth.   You open your *lips* when you speak and eat.

liquid *Liquid* runs or flows or pours.   Water, milk and lemonade are *liquids*.

listen When you *listen* you try to hear things.

little *Little* is small.   A *little* is not very much.

live (This *live* rhymes with give.) To *live* is to breathe and be full of life.

To *live* is also to be at home somewhere.   Americans *live* in America.

Red Riding Hood's grandmother *lived* in a cottage in the wood.

live (This *live* rhymes with five.)   *Live* is alive.   *Live* is not dead.   *Lively* is full of life and bounce and busyness.

load A *load* is something that is carried.   A *load* is often big or heavy.

The third Little Pig built his house with a *load* of bricks.

loaf A *loaf* is bread baked into a shape.   *Loaves* can be square or round or long and thin.

lock A *lock* is a fastening on a door, a gate, a drawer or a box.   You turn a key one way to *lock* and another way to *unlock*.

log A *log* is a thick, round piece of wood without branches or leaves. It is cut from a tree.

lollipop A *lollipop* is a big sweet on a little stick.

long *Long* is going on or stretching a great way, like a *long* road.

Long is lasting much time, like Sleeping Beauty's *long, long* sleep.

look To *look* is to use your eyes to see things.
  To *look after* is to take care of and be good to something or somebody.

loop A *loop* is an oval shape in string or in shoelaces when you tie them in a bow.

loose *Loose* is not tied or shut in. *Loose* is free.   *Loose* is not tight, like a *loose*, cool shirt.

lose If you *lose* a thing you cannot find it.   You do not have it any more. Cinderella *lost* one glass slipper. The Babes in the Wood *lost* their way.

lot A *lot* is a great many.
  A *lot* is a large number.
  A *lot* is very much.

loud *Loud* is noisy.
  'Fee fi fo fum
  I smell the blood of an Englishman
  the giant roared *loudly*.

love To like very, very much is to *love*.

lovely *Lovely* is beautiful.   *Lovely* is very, very pretty.

low *Low* is near the ground.   *Low* is not high or tall.

Low is quiet and soft, like your voice when you do not want everybody to hear you.

luck *Luck* is something that happens by chance.   *Good luck* is a happy happening you are *lucky* to have.

luggage *Luggage* is bags and cases and trunks filled with all you need for a journey.   *Luggage* is also called baggage.

Look at his **luggage**! Not his **lucky** day.

lunch *Lunch* is a meal eaten in the middle of the day.

M m

machine A *machine* moves and works and makes things more quickly and more easily than we can. Cars and washing machines and typewriters are kinds of *machines*.

magazine A *magazine* is pages full of short pieces of writing, pictures and photographs fastened together in soft paper covers.
 Some *magazines* come out every week and some every month.

magic *Magic* is the wonderful and strange things that happen in fairy stories – like a mirror that talks and a giant that turns into a mouse.
 Magic tricks are the quick, clever tricks of a quick, clever showman.

mail *Mail* is letters and parcels you send by the Post Office.

make To *make* is to build and shape and put things together.
 The first Little Pig *made* his house with straw.

male A *male* is a man or a boy.
 The *male* of a cow is a bull.

man A *man* is a boy who has grown up. *Men* are adult males.

many *Many* is a lot. *Many* is not just a few but a large number.

map A *map* is a drawing to show the shape of the world or a country.
 On a *map* you can find towns and rivers and hills and roads.

March *March* is the third month of the year. It has 31 days.

margarine *Margarine* is a food like butter for spreading and cooking. It is made from vegetable oils.

mark A *mark* is a line, a spot, a stain or a scratch.

A *mark* is a sign like × or * or ● to show you something.

market A *market* is little open shops called stalls, often in the open air, where all sorts of things are bought and sold.

marmalade *Marmalade* is jam made with oranges or lemons.

marry A man and a woman *marry* to be husband and wife.
 Both Cinderella and Snow White *married* princes.

marvellous   *Marvellous* is wonderful and surprising and exciting.

mask   A *mask* is a funny or a frightening cover to hide the face.

mast   A *mast* is the tall pole on a ship that holds the sails.   Flags fly from a *mast*.

mat   A *mat* is a rug or a small piece of carpet on the floor.
You wipe your shoes on a *doormat*.
You put a hot plate of food on a *table mat*.

match   A *match* is a thin stick with a tip that burns.

To *match* is to be the same size and colour, like two shoes for your two feet.   To *match* is to go together, like a red hat and red shoes.

A *match* is a game played between two people or two teams.   Each one tries to win.

material   A *material* is what a thing is made of.   Clothes are made of cloth.   Books are made of paper.

May   *May* is the fifth month of the year.   It has 31 days.

maybe   *Maybe* is perhaps.   *Maybe* the sun will shine tomorrow.   *Maybe* it will snow.   You cannot be sure.

meal   Breakfast is a *meal*.   Lunch and dinner are *meals*.   A *meal* is what you eat at those times.

mean   *Mean* is not nice.   *Mean* is not kind.
Cinderella's ugly sisters were *mean*.

To *mean* is to think and say you will do something.
The wicked wolf *meant* to have the Little Pig for dinner.

A dictionary tells you what words *mean*.   It tells you what they say and how to know and use them.

measles   You do not feel well and you have little red spots on your skin if you have *measles*.

meat   *Meat* is food from animals, like pork and beef and mutton.

medal   Round like a coin or in the shape of a cross, a *medal* is a prize for being very brave or very clever or very good.

medicine   If you are sick *medicine* helps to make you better.   You can sip it in spoonfuls or swallow a pill.

meet   When people *meet* they come together and say hello.
    When two walls or two streets *meet*, they come together at a corner.

melon   A *melon* is a big, juicy fruit with thick yellow or green skin and hundreds of little seeds in the middle.

melt   When the sun shines snow and ice will *melt*.   The sun's heat turns them to water.

mend   To *mend* is to put a thing right if it is broken or has a hole in it or just will not work.

merry   *Merry* is jolly and bright and full of fun.

mess   It is untidy, it is dirty and everything is mixed up.   It is a *mess*.

metal   *Metal* is hard and bright.   It is dug out of the ground and used to make all sorts of things, from cars to tools to jewellery.   Iron and steel and gold and silver are *metals*.

midday   Twelve o'clock noon is *midday*.   It is the middle of the day.

middle   The *middle* is halfway.   The *middle* is the centre.   Wednesday is the *middle* of the week.

midnight   Twelve o'clock at night is *midnight*.

milk   *Milk* is the white liquid mothers give their babies to drink.
    We drink cow's and goat's *milk*.

million   A *million* is 1 000 000.   A *million* is a thousand thousands.   A *millionaire* is a very rich person.

mind   Your *mind* is what you think with.

To *mind* is to look after.

To *mind* is to be careful.

mine   'It's *mine*,' cried each ugly sister in turn, trying to push a foot into the glass slipper.   'It belongs to me,' they both cried.

A *mine* is a big, very deep hole in the ground where *miners* dig out coal or gold or diamonds.

minibus   A *minibus* is a little bus with seats for about ten people.

minute   A *minute* is sixty seconds. There are sixty *minutes* in one hour.

mirror   '*Mirror, mirror* on the wall, who is the fairest of them all?' the wicked queen asked.   And who did she see in the looking glass?

mischief   *Mischief* is naughtiness and playing silly tricks.

miss   If you *miss* the bus you are not there to get it.
If you *miss* a ball you do not hit it or catch it.
If you *miss* a person you are sad to be without him.
If a thing is *missing*, it is lost.

Miss is also a girl or a woman who is not married.

mist   *Mist* is thin white-grey fog.

mistake   You make a *mistake* if you do or say something not quite right.

66

mix   *Mix* sugar and fruit to make jam. Two different things are put together.   Green is a *mixture* of blue and yellow.

moment   A *moment* is a very, very short time, like the time it takes to blink an eye.

Monday   *Monday* is the second day of the week.   *Monday* is usually the first working and school day of the week.

money   *Money* buys things.   *Money* is metal coins and paper banknotes.

monkey   A *monkey* is a small, furry animal with a long tail.   It lives among the trees and swings easily from branch to branch.

monster   A *monster* is a huge, fearsome, ugly thing, often half man and half animal.   You often find *monsters* in story books.

month   A *month* is one of the twelve parts of the year, like January or June.

moon   The *moon* is the bright light seen in the sky at night.   Sometimes it is full and round, sometimes thin like a slice of melon.

more   *More* is greater than.   Two is *more* than one.   It is one *more*. Snow White was *more* beautiful than the wicked queen.   Her beauty was greater.

morning   *Morning* is the first part of the day.   From dawn until midday is *morning*.

most   *Most* is the greatest or biggest. *Most* is nearly all.

mother   A *mother* is a woman with a child or children of her own.

motor   The *motor* is the engine that makes a machine work or move. A *motor car*, a *motorcycle*, a *motorboat* need *motors* to make them go.

motorway   A *motorway* is a wide main road for fast one-way driving.

Will man or **mouse** reach the top of the **mountain**?

mountain   A *mountain* is a very high hill, often rocky and steep and difficult to climb.

mouse   A *mouse* is a very little animal with sharp teeth and a long tail. *Mice* live in *mouseholes* in walls and floors.

mouth   Your *mouth* is below your nose and above your chin.   You open and shut your *mouth* when you speak and eat.

move   You *move* when you walk, run, crawl, jump or make any *movement* at all.

You *move* when you go to a new place to live.

You *move* things when you put them somewhere else.

much   *Much* is a lot.   *Too much* is more than you want or more than you need.

mud   *Mud* is soft, sticky earth full of water.   *Mud* makes your shoes *muddy*.

mug   A *mug* is a big cup with a handle. You get more to drink with a *mugful*.

mummy   *Mummy* and *mum* are family names for mother.

mumps   You do not feel well if you have *mumps*.   Your throat hurts and your neck swells.

music   *Music* is the tuneful sound of *musical* instruments playing or voices singing.

must   You *must* turn the pages to finish a story.   You have to.   You need to.

N n

nail   Hit a *nail* on the head with a hammer and its sharp point will join two pieces of wood together.

A *nail* is the hard tip that grows at the end of a finger or toe.

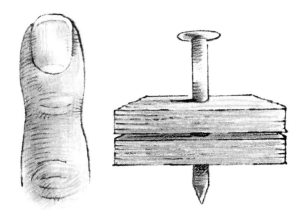

name   Your *name* is what you are called.   Everything in the world has a *name* that it is known by.

narrow   *Narrow* is not wide.   *Narrow* is thin and not far from side to side.

nasty   *Nasty* is not pleasant.   *Nasty* is not nice to taste or to smell.

naughty   Sometimes children and puppies are *naughty*.   They do not behave very well.   They are full of mischief.

near   *Near* is not far.   *Near* is close by, like neighbours.   *Nearly* is almost but not quite.

neat   *Neat* is tidy.

neck   Your *neck* joins your head to your shoulders.   A collar and tie fit round the *neck*.

A *necklace* is a string of jewels or pretty beads to wear round the *neck*.

nectar   *Nectar* is the sweet liquid bees suck from flowers to make honey.

need   You *need* a spade to dig a hole. You must have one.

If you *need* money you do not have any to spend.

needle   Made of shiny steel a *needle* is very thin, has a sharp point and a little eye for thread to go through. *Needles* are for sewing.

neighbour   A *neighbour* is someone who lives very near to you.

nephew   A *nephew* is the son of a brother or sister.

nest   A bird builds a *nest* for itself and its babies with twigs and grasses and fallen leaves.

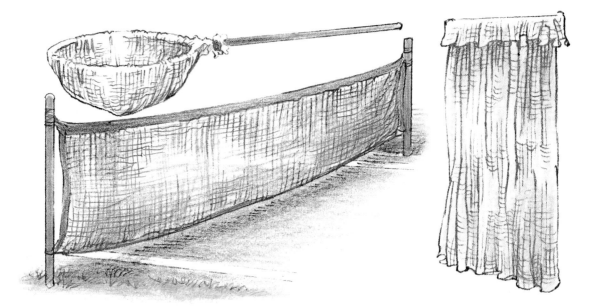

net *Net* is made of string or rope or thread or wire knotted together with lots of holes between. *Fishing nets, tennis nets*, dresses and curtains are some of the things made of *net*.

never *Never* is not at all, not even once. *Never* is not at any time.

new *New* is not old. *New* is fresh, just bought or just made, like *newly* baked bread.

news If it is *news* it is something that has just happened.
A *newspaper* comes out every day and tells you the latest, *newest* happenings.

next *Next* is nearest, like your *next-door* neighbour.
Next is the one after. The *next* word on this page is 'nice'.

nice *Nice* is pleasant and kind and good and helpful.

niece A *niece* is the daughter of a brother or sister.

night *Night is* the time between sunset and sunrise when the sky is dark.

nine *Nine* is 9. It is one more than eight. *Ninteeen* is 19. Ten and *nine* are *nineteen*. *Ninety* is 90. *Ninety* is ten times *nine*.

nobody Goldilocks knocked at the Bears' door but there was *nobody* there. Not anyone at all.

noise A *noise* is a sound. It is usually a loud sound like CRASH, BANG, BOOM or a giant's *noisy* roar.

none *None* is not any.
Goldilocks ate all Baby Bear's porridge and there was *none* left.

nonsense *Nonsense* is silly talk or silly writing that does not mean anything at all.

noon *Noon* is twelve o'clock midday.

north *North* is opposite south.
The *north* of a country is at the highest or top part of a map.

nose   You breathe and smell with your *nose.*   Your *nose* is in the middle of your face.

note   A *note* is a short little letter.
A *note* is written down in a *notebook* to tell you something or to help you remember.

A *note* is a paper *banknote.*

A *note* is one of the sounds when music is played.

nothing   *Nothing* is not anything at all.   If you have *nothing* in your pocket, your pocket is empty.

notice   To *notice* is to see.
A *notice* tells you something.   It is written for you to see.
NO WOLVES ALLOWED said the *notice* on the Little Pig's house.

November   *November* is the eleventh month of the year.   It has 30 days.

now   *Now* is not before.   *Now* is not after.   *Now* is at this very moment.

nowhere   *Nowhere* is not anywhere, not one place or another.   If you are going *nowhere*, you are staying right here.

number   How many Little Pigs are there in the story?   The *number* is three.   *Number* is the word that tells you how many.

nurse   If you are sick a *nurse* helps a doctor to look after you.

nut   A *nut* is a fruit with a hard shell, like a *chestnut*, a *walnut* and a *peanut.* You can eat the seed or fruit inside the shell.

Three happy Little Pigs like **nuts** for lunch.
Let's hope the wolf will **notice** the **notice**!

O o

oak From a little acorn, the *oak* grows into a very big tree. Its hard wood makes strong doors and furniture.

oar An *oar* is for rowing. It is a long pole with a flat end to dip in the water and pull a rowing boat along.

obey You do what someone tells you to do when you *obey*. You are *obedient*.

ocean An *ocean* is a very big sea, like the *Atlantic Ocean* between Britain and America. There are five *oceans* in the world.

October *October* is the tenth month of the year. It has 31 days.

office An *office* is a room to work in, usually at a desk.

often *Often* is not just sometimes but many, many times.

oil *Oil* is a thick, sticky liquid we get from animals and plants and from under the ground and under the sea.

old *Old* is not new, like *old* shoes you have worn for a long time.
  Old is not young, like Red Riding Hood's grandmother who had lived for a long time.

once *Once* is only one time.
  At one o'clock the clock strikes *once*.

  Once is not now. *Once* is at a time that is past. It is long ago.
  Dinosaurs *once* lived on the earth.

one *One* is 1. It is *one* more than nothing.

onion An *onion* is a vegetable, round like a bulb, with a strong taste and a strong smell.

only *Only* is one. *Only* is no more. Jack was an *only* child. He had no brothers or sisters.

open *Open* is not shut.   An *open* door lets you pass through.   An *open* window lets fresh air blow through.
In the open is out of doors in the *open* air.
An *opening* is a hole or a space or a way in.

opposite *Opposite* is on the other side.   *Opposite* is face to face.

Opposite means not the same at all.   *Opposite* is very different.   The *opposite* of big is small.

orange An *orange* is a round, juicy fruit with a bright red-yellow skin.

Orange is also the bright colour you get when you mix red and yellow together.

orchard Fruit trees all growing together are an *orchard*, like the apple *orchard* the Little Pig visited.

order An *order* tells you to do things. An *order* should be obeyed.

Order is neatness and tidiness and everything in its right place.

ordinary *Ordinary* is not different or special or exciting or new.
Ordinary is everyday and usual.

ostrich An *ostrich* is the biggest bird of all, but it cannot fly.   It has a long, thin neck and runs very fast on its long thin legs.

other *Other* is different.   *Other* is not the same.
Cinderella went home with only one slipper.   The *other* she lost on the way.

out *Out* is not in.
Out is not at home, like the Three Bears.

outside When you are *outside* you are not inside. You are in the open air.

oval An *oval* is a shape that is not quite round. An egg is *oval* in shape.

oven An *oven* is the part of the cooker to roast and bake food. It has a door to shut in the heat.

over *Over* is above. *Over* is on top. An *overcoat* goes on top of your clothes.

Over is past. *Over* is finished. Dick Whittington's journey was *over* when he got to London.

owl An *owl* is a night bird with a little hooked beak and big, round eyes.

own To *own* is to have a thing that is yours. It belongs to you and nobody else.

Dick Whittington had a cat of his *own*. He was its *owner*.

P p

pack To *pack* is to put things together into a bag or a case or a box.

A *pack* is a bag you fill with things and carry on your back.

packet A little parcel wrapped up to give or to send is a *packet* or a *package*.

paddle A *paddle* is a short oar to send a canoe through the water.

To *paddle* is to walk and splash in shallow water.

page A *page* is one of the sheets of paper that make up a book, a magazine or a newspaper.
This *page* is full of words and pictures.

pail A *pail* is a bucket. It holds water and has a handle to carry it.

pain A part of you hurts if you have a *pain*.
If you bump your head or cut your finger it is *painful*.

paint *Paint* is liquid colour to brush onto walls and wood.
An artist *paints* pictures with brushes and colours.

pair Two things that go together make a *pair*, like a *pair* of gloves for your two hands.

palace A king or a queen or a prince lives in a large, grand house called a *palace*.

pan A *pan* is a wide pot for cooking. A *frying pan* is a shallow *pan* with a long handle for frying things like eggs and pancakes.

pancake A *pancake* is a thin, flat cake fried on both sides in a frying pan.

panda A *panda* is an animal that looks like a little black and white bear.

paper Rags and wood help to make sheets of *paper* to write on, to print on, to paint on, to stick on walls, to wrap presents in.

Help! cries the **parrot** as the **parachute** floats past him.

parachute   A *parachute* is a big cloth umbrella strapped to a man to let him float safely to earth from an aeroplane.

parcel   Wrap a thing in paper, tie it with string or stick it with tape and it's a *parcel.*

parent   A mother or a father is a *parent.*

park   In town a *park* is a big, green open-air place where lawns and trees and flowers grow.   You can walk and picnic in the *park* and have fun in the children's playground.

To *park* a car is to stop and leave it for a time.

parrot   A *parrot* is a bird of hot lands with bright feathers of many colours and a hooked beak.   *Parrots* can copy sounds and words.

part   A *part* is a bit or a piece.   A branch is *part* of a tree.   Your nose is *part* of your face.

To *part* is to leave.   To *part* is to say goodbye.

party   It's fun and games and nice food for everybody at a *party.*

pass   To *pass* is to go by or move on.   Time *passes* every minute.

To *pass* is to go fast enough to get in front.

To *pass* is to hand a thing to someone.

passenger   A *passenger* takes a ride in a car, a bus, a train, a boat, an aeroplane.   A *passenger* is not the driver.

past   *Past* is gone or finished or over.
Yesterday is *past*, tomorrow is still to come.

When you run *past*, you do not stop, you go on running.

pastry   Flour and water and fat mixed together make *pastry*.   It is rolled flat and baked into tarts and pies.

pat   To touch or tap gently is to *pat*.

patch   A little piece of cloth sewn over a hole or a tear is a *patch*.
A little bit of ground is a *patch*, like a *patch* of grass or a *cabbage patch*.

path   A *path* is a narrow track or a way to walk on.

pattern   Lines or shapes drawn over and over again make a *pattern*.

pavement   A *pavement* is the hard path at the side of the road where you can walk safely.   It is the footpath or the sidewalk.

paw   A *paw* is the foot of an animal with claws, like a cat or a dog or a lion.

pay   You give money to *pay* for something you buy.   People are *paid* money for the work they do.   It is their *pay* or their *payment*.

pea   A *pea* is a little round, green seed that grows in a pod.   We cook *peas* or eat them raw.

peace   *Peace* is quietness and stillness.   There is no noise and no fighting.   It is *peaceful*.
Peace is a time without war.

peach   A *peach* is a soft, sweet, juicy fruit with a stone in the middle.   Its skin is pink-yellow and feels like fine, silky hair.

pear   A *pear* is a juicy fruit, green or yellow, round at the bottom and pointed at the top.

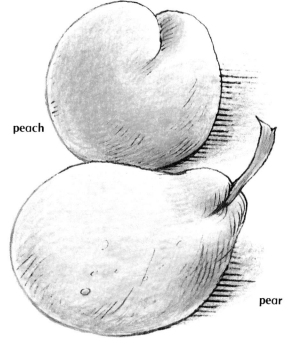

peach

pear

pebble   A *pebble* is a nearly round, smooth little stone found on a stony beach.

peck Birds take quick little bites when they *peck* food with their beaks.

pedal You make a machine move if you press a *pedal* with your foot.

peep You take a quick look when you *peep* or *peek*.
  Jack *peeped* out of the oven to make sure the giant was asleep.

pen You hold a *pen* in your hand to write or draw with ink.

pencil You write and draw with a *pencil*. It is usually made of wood with a black or coloured strip inside.
  A *pencil sharpener* makes a fine, sharp point on a *pencil*.

penguin A *penguin* is a black and white bird that does not fly. It swims in the icy waters round the cold lands of the south.

penny A *penny* is a small brown metal coin. One hundred *pennies* or *pence* make a pound.

people *People* are persons. *People* are a lot of men, women and children.
  The *people* of the world are everybody.

pepper *Pepper* gives a hot, sharp taste to food. *Pepper* comes from the ripe berries of the *pepper plant*.
  Red peppers and *green peppers* are big, shiny vegetables that grow in hot lands.

perhaps *Perhaps* is maybe. Maybe yes and maybe no; you cannot be sure.

person Everyone is a *person*. You are a *person* and each man and woman and child in the world is a *person* too.

pet A *pet* is an animal you like and look after at home. Dogs and cats are favourite *pets*.

petal A *petal* is one of the coloured parts of a flower. *Petals* grow from the centre of a flower.

petrol *Petrol* is the liquid that makes cars go. It is poured into the *petrol tank*. *Petrol* is sometimes called gasoline.

photograph A *photograph* is a picture taken with a camera.

piano A *piano* is a musical instrument with black and white keys for your fingers to press to make music.

pick To *pick* is to choose.
Out of all the fine ladies at the ball, the prince *picked* Cinderella.

To *pick* is to gather flowers or fruit.
Red Riding Hood *picked* flowers in the wood.

picnic You eat in the open air when you have a *picnic*. You can take a trip to the country, the seaside or the park to *picnic*.

picture A *picture* is a drawing or a painting or a photograph.

pie It has pastry below and pastry on top and meat or fruit in the middle. Bake it in a hot oven and it's a *pie*.

piece A *piece* is a bit. A *piece* of pie is a part of the pie.

pier At the seaside a *pier* is built out over the water like a long railway platform. Boats tie up at the *pier*. You can walk on the *pier* and fish from the *pier*.

pig A *pig* is a farm animal with thick, hairy skin and a little curly tail. Bacon, ham and pork come from the *pig*.

pigeon A *pigeon* is a bird with a little head, a fat body and short legs. Some *pigeons* live in towns, some in the woods and some are kept as racing pets.

pile A *pile* is a heap. A *pile* is a lot of things built up one on top of the other.

pill A *pill* is a little bit of medicine to swallow. It can be flat or round or shaped like an egg.

pillow A *pillow* is a soft cushion to rest your head on in bed.

pilot A *pilot* flies an aeroplane and steers it through the sky.
A sailor who guides a ship into port is a *pilot* too.

A **pilot** steers for the **pier**.

pin   A *pin* fastens things together.   It is a little piece of thin very shiny metal with a sharp point and a tiny head.

pink   *Pink* is a colour between white and red.   It is light red like the sky at dawn.

pipe   A *pipe* is a long tube to bring water or gas or oil from place to place.
    A *pipe* for smoking has a thin tube at one end and a little bowl at the other.
    A *pipe* for playing music is a thin tube with little holes in it like the *pipe* the Pied Piper blew.

pirate   A *pirate* on a *pirate ship* robs other ships at sea.

pit   A *pit* is a big, deep hole in the ground.   Miners dig coal from a *coal pit*.

pizza   A *pizza* is flat and round like a tart.   It has soft pastry on the bottom and cheese and tomatoes or ham or lots of other tasty things on top.

place   A *place* is a special spot where a thing or a person stands or sits.   A kitchen is the *place* for a cooker. People take their *places* in a queue.
    A *place* is also the town or the village or the country where you live.
    To *place* is to put a thing where you want it to be.

planet   Earth is a *planet* in the sky.   It goes round the sun and is lit by the sun.   There are eight more *planets* in the sky.

plant   A *plant* grows from roots in the earth.   Some *plants* grow in water.
    To *plant* is to put *plants* or seeds or bulbs in the earth or a pot and watch them grow.

plastic   *Plastic* is a material made by man.   It is used instead of metal or wood or leather or glass to make lots of things like toys and buckets and dishes and waterproofs.

plate   A *plate* is a flat dish to put food on and to eat food from.

platform   A *platform* is higher than the floor.   It is a raised floor where speakers speak or bands play to an audience.

At the railway station a *platform* is beside and above the rails.   Trains stop at the *platform*.

play   You do not work when you *play*. You have fun and *play* games.

To *play* is to make music on a musical instrument.

A *play* is a story *players* act on the stage.

playground   A *playground* is a place to play out of doors at school or in the park.

please   To *please* is to make someone happy and glad.

You say '*please*' when you ask for something politely.
'*Please* may I eat from your plate?' said the Frog Prince to the princess.
The princess did not think this *pleasant* or nice.   She was not at all *pleased*.

plenty   *Plenty* is not just enough.   *Plenty* is more than enough.   *Plenty* is lots.

plough   A farmer cuts the earth and turns it over with the sharp blades of his *plough*.   A tractor or sometimes a horse pulls the *plough*.

pluck   To *pluck* is to pull with the fingers the strings of a musical instrument.
To *pluck* is to pull ripe fruit from a fruit tree.

plum   A *plum* is a juicy fruit, purple, yellow or green with one stone inside.

pocket   It is handy to have a *pocket* or two sewn into your clothes.   A *pocket* is like a little bag to hold little things.

pod   A *pod* is a case that holds the seeds of some plants.   Peas and beans have *pods*.

poem   A *poem* is lines of writing that tell the thoughts of a *poet* in beautiful sounding words.   *Poems* are often in rhyme.

point   A *point* is a tiny spot.

A *point* is a sharp tip like the *point* of a needle, an arrow or a sharp pencil.

To *point* is to show something with your finger.   A signpost *points* the way to a place.

pole   A *pole* is a long, strong post to hold things high.
A *flagpole* holds up a flag.
Clothes poles hold up a *clothes rope*.

police   The *police* are *policemen* and *policewomen* who help to keep the laws of the country.

polite   You say and do things nicely when you are *polite*.   You are pleasant and well behaved.

pond   In a park or a garden, a *pond* is a little lake of quiet water.   A *pond* can be a *fishpond*, a *duckpond*, a *boating pond*.

pony   A *pony* is a little horse.

pool   The princess's golden ball fell into a deep *pool*.   A *pool* is a piece of quiet water in a river or a stream.
    A *swimming pool* is a special pond built to swim in.

poor   *Poor* is not rich.   *Poor* is without much money.

porridge   *Porridge* is food made with seeds of grass called oats, and water or milk.   It is eaten hot for breakfast.
    Whose *porridge* did Goldilocks eat?

port   A *port* or a *seaport* is a big town by the sea with a *port* or harbour for ships.

porter   A *porter* carries your luggage at a railway station or a hotel.

post   The *post* is the mail.   The *post* is letters and parcels and packets you send by the *Post Office* or drop into a *postbox*.
    The *Post Office* takes in mail and sends it out.   You buy stamps at the *Post Office*.
    The *postman/woman* brings your *post* in a *postbag*.

   A *post* is a pole, short or long that stands straight up in the ground, like a *lamp post* or *gate posts* that hold up a gate.

postcard   A *postcard* is a thin card to write on and send by the Post Office.   *Postcards* often have a pretty or a funny picture on one side.

pot   A *pot* is a dish with a lid and a handle to cook food in.

potato   A *potato* is a vegetable you dig out of the ground.   It has a brown or a red skin.   You can boil it or bake it or cut it into chips.

pound   A *pound* is money.   A *pound* is 100 pence.

   A *pound* is weight.   How many *pounds* do you weigh?   Step on the scales and find out.

pour   When you *pour* tea you let it run out of the teapot and into a cup.
    When it *pours* with rain, it is not just a shower.   Rain falls hard and fast from the sky.

powder   *Powder* is as fine, as soft and as tiny as dust or flour or tiny snowflakes.

pram   A *pram* is a little bed on wheels for a baby who cannot walk yet.

precious   *Precious* is very much loved or very dear.

    Precious is very valuable like a *precious* jewel.   Diamonds are *precious* jewels.

present   A *present* is for giving.
    Puss in Boots took a *present* of rabbits to the castle.   He gave them to the king.

    You are *present* if you are here. You are not absent.

press   To *press* is to push.   You *press* some door bells with your finger.
    To *press* is to squeeze.
    To *press* is to make clothes flat and smooth with a hot iron.

pretend   To *pretend* is to be or say you are someone you are not.
    The wicked wolf *pretended* to be Red Riding Hood's grandmother.

pretty   *Pretty* is lovely to look at, like a *pretty* flower or a *pretty* picture.

price   The *price* is the money you must pay to buy a thing.

prick   To *prick* is to make a little hole with a sharp little point, like a *pinprick*.
    Prickly is covered in sharp little points, like a hedgehog's back.
    If you touch a *prickly* thing your skin stings.

prince   A *prince* is the son of a king or a queen.

Puss in Boots brings **presents** to the king.

Too much **pudding** will make a fat **princess**.

princess A *princess* is the daughter of a king or a queen.

print You are looking at *print* on this page. It is the letters and the pictures a machine has pressed onto the paper.
A *printer* looks after a *printing machine*.

prison *Prison* is a place where people who do not obey the law are locked up.

prize A *prize* is a reward, or a present for being the best or the cleverest.

programme A *programme* is all the things you will see and hear at a show or a concert or a circus.
A *programme* on radio or television is one of lots of things to listen to or watch at special times.

promise To *promise* is to say you will be sure to do something.
To keep your *promise* is to do what you say you will do.

pudding You eat *pudding* at the end of a meal. *Pudding* is sweet and soft and hot or sweet and cold.

puddle A *puddle* is a little pool of water left after heavy rain.

pull To *pull* is to draw or to tug.
Six white horses *pulled* Cinderella's coach behind them.
You *pull* hard on a rope in a game of tug o' war.
Pull is the opposite of push.

pumpkin A *pumpkin* is a big round fruit that grows on the ground. It has thick orange skin, is soft inside and has lots of seeds.

pupil A *pupil* is a boy or a girl at school. A *pupil* learns what a teacher teaches.

puppet A *puppet* is a doll on strings. It moves and dances when the strings are pulled. A *puppet* on your hand moves with your fingers.

puppy   A *puppy* is a young dog.

purple   *Purple* is the colour of ripe grapes and plums.   *Purple* is the rich colour you get when you mix red and blue together.

purr   Cats *purr* when they are happy. They make a soft low growl in their throats.

purse   A *purse* is a little bag for money.

push   To *push* is to move by pressing against something.
   Push is the opposite of pull.

put   To *put* is to place.   To *put* is to lay a thing where you want it to be.

puzzle   It is hard to find the answer to a *puzzle*.   You must think and wonder and think again.
   A *jigsaw puzzle* is fun to work out and fit together.

pyjamas   *Pyjamas* are a jacket and trousers to wear in bed.

Do you like doing a **jigsaw puzzle** in **purple pyjamas**?

Q q

quarrel   A *quarrel* is angry talk between people.   They *quarrel* because they do not think the same about something.

quarter   There are four *quarters* in a whole.   A *quarter* is half of a half.   A *quarter* is ¼.

queen   A *queen* rules a country.   She is her country's first lady.   A *queen* is also the wife of a king.

question   A *question* is what you ask when you want to know something. You want an answer.
   'Where are you taking your cow?' was the old man's *question*.
   'To market,' was Jack's answer.

queue   A *queue* is a long line of people or traffic waiting to go somewhere.

quick   *Quick* is fast.   *Quick* is clever and *quick* to learn.   *Quickly* is as fast as you can.
   Quickly is in a hurry, like Jack running from the giant.

quiet   Not a sound is heard when it is *quiet*.   It is still and peaceful.   When you speak *quietly* you speak softly. You do not shout.

How many people are waiting in the bus **queue**?

R r

rabbit   A *rabbit* is a little animal with a furry coat, long ears and a short little tail.

race   You run as fast as you can when you *race*.   In a *race* the fastest runner or car or horse is the winner.

racket   A *racket* is an oval bat with springy strings to play tennis.

radio   A *radio* sends and brings voices, music and sounds through the air by electricity.

raft   A *raft* is flat and floats on water.   It is made of logs tied together.

rag   A *rag* is an old torn piece of cloth.   *Rags* are old clothes, like Cinderella's as she sat by the fire.

railway   Long bars of metal are the *rails* of the *railway* track.   Trains run on the *rails*.

rain   *Rain* is water falling from the clouds on a *rainy* day.   A *raincoat* keeps you dry when it *rains*.

rainbow   A *rainbow* is a curve of seven colours in the sky when the sun shines through a shower of rain.

raise   To *raise* is to lift up.   *Raised* is built higher, like a platform or a stage.

rake   A *rake* is a garden tool with teeth and a long handle.   It gathers hay or leaves or loose grass into heaps.

raspberry   A *raspberry* is a soft little red fruit full of seeds.

rat   A *rat* is an animal with sharp teeth and a long, thin tail.   It looks like a big mouse.

raw   *Raw* food is not cooked food.

ray   A *ray* is a long, narrow line of bright light like a sunbeam.

reach   To *reach* is to get to the place you want to go.   After a long climb, Jack *reached* the top of the beanstalk.   He arrived at last.

To *reach* is also to stretch up or down or over.

read　You look at words and know what they mean when you *read*.
　Dick Whittington *read* TO LONDON on the signpost and understood what it said.　(This *read* rhymes with said.)

ready　When everything you need to do first is done, you are *ready*.

real　*Real* is true.　*Real* is not make-believe.

record　A *record* is a round, black, very thin plate or disc to play on a *record player*.　It plays words and music for you to listen to.

recorder　A *recorder* is a musical instrument like a pipe to blow and make music.

red　*Red* is the bright colour of ripe cherries and tomatoes and Red Riding Hood's hood.

refrigerator　A *refrigerator* is a special ice box with shelves and a door.　It keeps food cold and fresh.

reindeer　A *reindeer* is a big deer that lives in the cold lands of the North.

remember　To *remember* is to hold things in your mind.　You do not forget the things you *remember*.

rest　To *rest* is to stop doing the thing you are doing.
　To *rest* is to be still and sometimes to sleep.

The *rest* is the people or things that are left.　The *rest* is the others.

restaurant　A *restaurant* is a place to eat and drink.　It is bigger than a café and waiters bring you your meal.

return　To come back is to *return*.
　Cinderella *returned* from the ball a few minutes after midnight.

To *return* is to give back, like something you have borrowed.

reward　A *reward* is a prize or a present for being good or clever.

rhinoceros　A *rhinoceros* is a very big, wild animal with very thick skin. Some have one horn, some have two horns.

rhyme   The beanstalk grew so very tall
Jack could not see the top at all.
'Tall' and 'all' are words that
rhyme.   They have the same sound.
A *rhyme* is also a whole poem with
lines that end in words that *rhyme*.

ribbon   A *ribbon* is a long, pretty strip of
fine cloth to tie round a parcel, a hat
or a girl's hair.   Loops or bows of
ribbon look pretty on a dress.

rice   *Rice* is a grass that grows in wet
ground in hot lands.   We cook and
eat its seeds.

rich   Thanks to the giant's gold, Jack and
his mother were *rich*.   They had lots
of money to spend.

A deep, bright colour like purple or
deep red is a *rich* colour.

riddle   A *riddle* is a funny puzzle
question with a funny answer.
Do you know what has teeth but
never bites?
A comb.

ride   To *ride* is to sit on something that
moves and travels, like a horse or a
bicycle.
The prince *rode* through the thick
forest to find Sleeping Beauty.

right   You have a *right* hand and a left
hand.   *Right* is the opposite of left.

Right is also true.   *Right* is not
wrong.

ring   A *ring* is round like a circle.   A *ring*
is round like an ○.
A *ring* is a pretty band of gold or
other metal on a finger.   Sometimes
precious stones shine on a *ring*.

A *ring* is the sound of a bell when it is
pressed, pulled or shaken.
The bells *rang* out on Cinderella's
wedding day.   They had *rung* since
sunrise.

ripe   *Ripe* fruit has stopped growing and
is ready to eat.
Ripe corn has turned golden and
ripened and is ready for cutting.

rise   To *rise* is to go up like a bird from a
branch, or an aeroplane from the
ground.
You *rise* when you stand up.

To *rise* is also to get up out of bed,
like you this morning.   Yesterday
you *rose* too.   You have *risen* every
day this week.

river   A *river* is fresh water flowing
between banks to the sea.

road   A *road* is a hard highway built to take traffic from one place to another.

roar   Big, wild animals like lions and tigers – and storybook giants too – *roar*.   They open their mouths and make loud, deep sounds in their throats.

roast   To *roast* is to cook meat in the oven.
   Roasted potatoes are good with *roast* meat.

rob   To *rob* is to steal.   A thief is a *robber*.
   A *robber* at sea is a pirate.

robot   A *robot* is a machine built to do things like a living person.

rock   A *rock* is a big, hard, heavy stone.   A mountain is *rocky* and the seashore may be *rocky*.   They are covered with great stones.

To *rock* is to move gently from side to side or to and fro like a *rocking chair*.

rocket   A *rocket* is a firework that shoots into the air with a bang.
   An astronaut shoots into space in a flying *rocket* shaped like a tube.

rod   A *rod* is a long, thin bar of wood or metal, like a *fishing rod*.

roll   To *roll* is to turn over and over like a *rolling* ball or great waves or *rollers* onto a beach.

To *roll* is to make flat like a lawn with a *roller* or pastry with a *rolling pin*.

A *roll* is a little loaf of bread just enough for one.

roof   A *roof* is the cover on top of a building or car.   A *roof* keeps out the rain.

room   A *room* is any part of the inside of a house or a flat with walls and a ceiling and a floor.   The kitchen, the *bathroom*, the *bedroom* are all *rooms*.

Room is space.
   There was lots of *room* for Jack to hide in the giant's huge oven.

root A plant or a tree grows from its *root* or *roots* under the ground.

rope *Rope* is made of very thick, very strong pieces of string or wire twisted together into a long, heavy line.
  Rope is for tying up and climbing up and swinging on.

rose A *rose* is a beautiful flower with petals of all colours and a sweet smell. Often its stem is prickly.

rough *Rough* is not smooth or flat.
  A *rough* road is stony and covered in bumps.
  A *rough* sea is wild and stormy.

round *Round* is shaped like a ring or a ball or a circle.

roundabout A *roundabout* or a merry-go-round is a moving circle of toys to ride on for fun at the fair.
  Traffic goes round a *roundabout* on the road. It is a big island in the middle where many roads meet.

row (This *row* rhymes with low.)
  A *row* is a long line, like a *row* of seats in the cinema.

To *row* is to drive a *rowing boat* along by dipping and pulling on the oars.

row (This *row* rhymes with now.)
  A *row* is a noisy quarrel.
  A *row* is a very loud noise.

rub To *rub* is to clean or scrub or make shiny with a brush or a duster.

rubber   *Rubber* tyres and *rubber* bands and *rubber* boots are made from a thick liquid in the *rubber tree*.

A *rubber* or eraser rubs out pencil marks on paper.

rubbish   Useless things are *rubbish*. They are broken or old or worn out or empty.

Rubbish is silly talk.   *Rubbish* is nonsense.

rude   *Rude* is not polite or pleasant or well behaved.

rug   A *rug* is a little carpet.   A *rug* is a mat on the floor.

A *rug* is a warm woolly blanket.

rule   Kings and queens *rule* their countries.   They are *rulers* or leaders.

A *rule* is a law.   A *rule* is an order that must be obeyed.

ruler   A *ruler* shows you how long a thing is.   It is a flat, straight wooden or metal stick with marks and numbers on it.

run   When you *run* you make your legs go very fast.

Goldilocks *ran* away from the Three Bears' house as fast as she could *run*.

rush   You move fast when you *rush* because you have to hurry.

S s

sack   A *sack* is a big, strong bag made of cloth, thick paper or plastic.
   Puss in Boots took a *sack* full of rabbits as a present to the king.

sad   *Sad* is not happy.
   Poor *sad* Cinderella sat weeping by the kitchen fire.

safe   *Safe* is away from danger, like the third Little Pig, *safe* from the wolf in his little brick house.

sail   To *sail* is to go places by boat or ship.   To *sail* is to steer or guide a boat.
   A *sailing boat* has *sails* to catch the wind and drive it over the water.   A *sailor sails* and works on a ship.

salad   *Salad* is vegetables with egg or meat or fish or rice all mixed together and eaten cold.
   Fruit salad is a mixture of sweet fruits and juices.

sale   FOR SALE says the notice.
   A *salesman* wants to sell this old house for money.   Who will buy it?

salt   *Salt* is found deep in the earth and in the sea.   It is rough, white powder and gives food a sharp, *salty* taste.

same   One pea looks very like another pea.   They look the *same*.   They do not look different.

sand   *Sand* is tiny, fine pieces of rock like rough yellow-grey powder on a *sandy* beach or in the desert.

sandal   A *sandal* is a light open shoe tied on with strips of leather across the foot and round the heel.

sandwich   Spread anything you like on a slice of bread.   Put a slice of bread on top and you have a *sandwich*.

Who would like a giant sausage and **salad sandwich**?

Saturday   *Saturday* is the seventh day of the week.   No school on *Saturday*!

sauce   *Sauce* is a tasty liquid to add taste to food.   Do you like tomato *sauce* with spaghetti?

saucer   A cup sits on a small, flat round dish called a *saucer*.

sausage   A *sausage* is chopped up meat in a thin skin to grill or to fry.

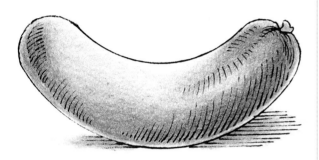

save   To *save* is to help someone out of danger.   To *save* is to make safe.

To *save* is also to keep things to use later.   If you *save* money you do not spend it.
Hansel *saved* his bread to drop on the path.

saw   A *saw* is a tool with teeth to cut through wood.

say   To *say* is to speak.   You use words when you *say* anything at all.   You will have *said* something.

scale   A *scale* is one of the very thin little plates on the bodies of fish.

scales   *Scales* are for weighing.   You can weigh food on *scales*.   You can weigh yourself on *scales*.

scare   To *scare* is to frighten.
Goldilocks was *scared* of the Three Bears.   She was very afraid.

scarf   A *scarf* is a long piece of cloth to wind round your neck on cold winter days.

school   At *school* you learn in class all the things that teachers teach.

scientist   A *scientist* works at finding out why and how everything in the world happens.

scissors   *Scissors* are two sharp blades fixed in the middle for cutting, with two finger holes to hold them. *Scissors* cut cloth and paper and hair.

scooter   A *scooter* is like a little motorcycle.   It has two wheels and an engine to drive it along.
A *scooter* for children has a board for one foot between two little wheels and a handle bar.   The other foot pushes it along.

scratch   A *scratch* is a mark or a cut left by something sharp like a nail.
Do you *scratch* with your fingernails when something tickles?

scream   To *scream* is to yell.   To *scream* is to give a loud, sharp cry.
    The wicked queen *screamed* with anger when she heard Snow White was alive.

screw   A *screw* is a special nail with little round cuts in it to fasten things together.
    A *screwdriver* turns a *screw* and makes it tight.

scrub   To *scrub* is to rub hard with a brush and soap and water.

sea   The *sea* is the salt water that covers a very large part of the Earth.
    The *seashore* is the edge of the *sea*.   It is the beach, sometimes sandy, sometimes covered in pebbles and *seashells* and rocks.

seal   A *seal* is a big sea animal with smooth furry skin.   It can also live on land.

season   A *season* is one of the four *seasons* of the year – spring, summer, autumn or fall and winter.

seat   A *seat* is something to sit on at home or outside or anywhere at all.

second   *Second* comes after first. Number 2 is the *second* number.

    A *second* is a very short time.   There are sixty *seconds* in one minute.

secret   A *secret* is something only you know.   *Secret* is hidden, like a *secret* drawer.

see   You *see* with your eyes.   You look at things.   You notice things.
    Hansel and Gretel *saw* a cottage made of sweets.   They had never *seen* so many sweets.

seed   If you plant a *seed* a new plant or a new tree will grow from it.

seek To *seek* is to look for. In a game of *hide-and-seek*, one player looks for the others who are hiding.

seesaw A *seesaw* is a long board fixed to a post in the middle. When one end is up the other is down. It is fun for two to swing on a *seesaw*.

sell Shops *sell* the things you want to buy. You give money for them. Jack *sold* his cow for a bag of magic beans instead of money.

send You *send* a letter by post. You make it go where you want it to go. Jack's angry mother *sent* him to bed. She made him go.

September *September* is the ninth month of the year. *September* has 30 days.

set To *set* is to put. To *set* is to place a thing where you want it to be.

A *set* is things that go together like the engine and coaches and rails in a train *set*.

seven *Seven* is 7. It is one more than six. *Seventeen* is 17. Ten and *seven* make *seventeen*. *Seventy* is 70. *Seventy* is ten times *seven*.

sew To *sew* is to make or to mend with a needle and thread. Cloth is cut into pieces and *sewn* together to make clothes.

shake To *shake* is to move quickly up and down, or to and fro. You *shake* your head to say 'no'. The leaves on the trees *shook* in the strong wind.

shallow *Shallow* water is not deep water. A plate is *shallow*, a bucket is deep.

shape The *shape* of a thing is what it looks like. The *shape* of a ball is round. Clay is *shaped* into pots and china. They are given their own *shapes*.

share The princess had to *share* her dinner with the Frog Prince. He had a part of it. He had some.

sharp A needle is *sharp*. It has a fine point. A knife is *sharp*. It has a fine edge that cuts.

sheep A *sheep* is a farm animal with a thick woolly coat and horns on its head.

sheet In bed you lie between cool cloth *sheets*. A thin piece of paper or glass is also called a *sheet*.

shelf A thin strong board fixed to a wall or inside a cupboard or a bookcase is a *shelf*. *Shelves* hold all kinds of things.

shell The hard outside of a nut or an egg is the *shell*. Some animals, like snails, and some insects have *shells*. *Seashells* on the seashore belong to little sea animals.

You *shell* peas when you crack open the pods.

A *shell* is shot from a big gun.

shepherd A *shepherd* looks after sheep with a sheepdog to help him.

shine To *shine* is to be as bright as sunlight on a sunny day. If you brush your shoes hard, they will be *shiny*.
The moon *shone* down on the sleeping Babes in the Wood.

ship A *ship* is a big boat that sails across the sea.

shirt A *shirt* is worn on the top part of the body. It has sleeves, short or long and a tail bit behind.

shiver You shake all over when you *shiver* with cold.

shoe You wear a *shoe* on each foot to have warm and dry feet.

shoot To *shoot* is to let fly at a target, bullets from a gun or arrows from a bow.

shop You buy things at a *shop*.
A *shopkeeper* sells the things you want.
The *shopping* is all the things you buy at the *shops*.

short *Short* is not long. *Short* is not tall.
A *short* journey does not take long. You arrive quite soon.

shoulder Your arm meets your body at your *shoulder*.

shout To *shout* is to cry out loudly. You want to be heard when you *shout* or yell.

show '*Show* me what you got for the cow,' said Jack's mother. And Jack let her see the bag of beans.

The signpost *showed* the way to London. It pointed it out.

A *show* is a film or a play to look at for fun.

It won't last long. It's just a **shower**!

shower   A *shower* is a quick short fall of rain or snow.
  Stand under a *shower* for a quick hot or cold *shower bath*.

shut   To *shut* is to close, like a door or a window.   *Shut* is not open, like your eyes when you sleep.

shy   *Shy* is a little afraid of people.   *Shy* is easily frightened.

sick   *Sick* is ill.   *Sick* is not feeling very well.

side   The *side* of the road is the edge. The left *side* of a thing is opposite the right *side* with the middle in between.   *Side by side* is beside or close together.   Your arms hang down by your *sides*.

sight   You can see things because you have *sight*.   *Sight* is seeing with your eyes.
  A *sight* is anything that your eyes can see.

sign   A *sign* tells you things without speaking words.   A shake of the head is a 'no' sign.
  A *sign* is a notice on a *signpost* to help or tell you things, like **STOP** or **TO THE SEA → I MILE.**

silent   *Silent* is quiet.   *Silent* is without a sound.
  When you are *silent* you do not say a word.   You keep *silence*.

silk   *Silk* is soft, smooth, fine cloth.
  Silkworms spin the fine threads to make silk.
  Silky is soft and smooth as *silk* or the skin of a peach.

silly   *Silly* is not very clever, like the Little Pig who built his house of straw.
  Silly is funny, like *silly* rhymes.

silver   *Silver* is a shiny white-grey precious metal.   Jewellery and money and forks and knives and spoons are made out of *silver*.
  Silver is also the bright white-grey colour of *silver*.

sing   Your voice makes music when you *sing*.   You make tuneful sounds.

single   *Single* is one and only one.

sink   A stone will *sink* in water.   It will not float.   It will go under.
   The princess's golden ball *sank* to the bottom of the pool.

   In the kitchen a *sink* is a big bowl with taps for washing things in.

sip   To *sip* is to drink a very little at a time.

sister   If you have a *sister* she is a girl with the same mother and father as you.

sit   To *sit* is to rest or be on a chair or a seat with your back nearly straight and your feet on the floor – if your legs are long enough.
   Goldilock *sat* on three chairs and broke one.

six   *Six* is 6.   It is one more than five. *Sixteen* is 16.   Ten and *six* make *sixteen*.   *Sixty* is 60.   *Sixty* is ten times *six*.

size   What *size* are you?   Your *size* is how big or how small you are.

skate   To *skate* is to slide smoothly over the ice on *skates*.
   Skates are fine blades of metal fixed to *skating boots*.
   You can *rollerskate* along the ground on little wheels fixed to boots.

ski   To *ski* is to slide fast over snow on *skis*.
   Skis are long narrow pieces of wood or metal fastened onto boots.

skin   *Skin* covers the whole of the outside of your body.
   Animals and fruits also have *skins*, some thin, some thick.

skip   On one leg then the other you spring lightly up and down as you *skip* along.
   You can jump like this over a *skipping rope* too.

skirt   Girls and women wear a *skirt*.   It hangs from the waist.
   A *skirt* is also the bottom half of a dress from the waist down.

sky   Up above the earth is the *sky*.   It is light in the daytime and dark at night.
A *skyscraper* is a very tall building rising up towards the *sky*.

slate   *Slate* is a smooth grey or blue-grey rock.   It is sliced into thin pieces for roofs and pavements and blackboards.

sledge (or **sled** or **sleigh**)   A *sledge* runs and slides smoothly over the snow on runners.
Big *sledges* are pulled by dogs or by horses.

sleep   You are not awake when you *sleep*.   You are *asleep* and resting with your eyes shut.
Sleeping Beauty slept for a hundred years.

sleeve   The *sleeve* of a shirt, a jacket or a jumper covers your arm.   You have two *sleeves* for your two arms.

slice   A *slice* is a thin, flat piece cut from anything that can be cut, like bread and cake and sausage and ham.

slide   To *slide* is to slip or move smoothly over ice and snow.
To *slide* is to move along easily, like *sliding doors*.
To *slide* is to slip and fall over.

slip   To *slip* is to slide.
To *slip* is to fall down when your feet slide away from you on a *slippery* floor.

To *slip* is to move quietly and quickly.

slipper   You wear a *slipper* on each foot.   *Slippers* are soft, light and warm to slip about in at home.

slow   *Slow* is not fast or quick.   A *slow* train takes a long time to arrive.
The giant moved too *slowly* to catch Jack.

small   *Small* is little.   *Small* is not big or fat or wide.

smart   *Smart* is quick and clever.
Smart is neat and tidy.

smell   You *smell* things with your nose.   It tells you what their *smells* are when you breathe them in. Sweet or sharp or bad or burned, most things *smell* of something.

smile   You *smile* with your lips when you are happy and pleased.

smoke   *Smoke* goes up like a black or blue-grey cloud when something burns.

smooth   *Smooth* is flat with no bends or curls.   *Smooth* is not rough. *Smooth* is silky like a cat's fur.
   To *smooth* is to make flat or press out the folds.

snail   A *snail* is a slow little garden animal with a curled shell on its back.

snake   A *snake* is a long thin animal without legs.   It twists and curls its body as it slides along the ground.

Will **snake** give **snail** a **smooth** ride?

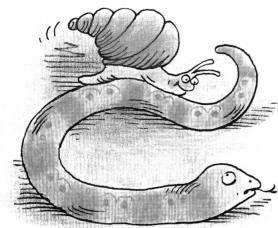

sneeze   A *sneeze* is a quick little burst of air from your nose when it tickles.

snow   *Snow* is drops of frozen rain that float down in a shower of white *snowflakes*.
   It is fun to make *snowballs* and build *snowmen* with *snow*.

soap   *Soap* is made from fats.   Sweet smells and colour are often added before you use it with water to wash.

sock   A *sock* is worn on each foot. *Socks* are short to cover the ankle or long and reach up to the knee.

sofa   A *sofa* is a long, soft couch for two or three people to sit on.

soft   *Soft* is not hard.   *Soft* is not rough. A *soft* cushion is nice to sit on.
   Soft is not loud.   *Soft* is quiet and gentle like a whisper or a light wind blowing *softly*.

soldier   A *soldier* is a person in an army.

some   *Some* is not all.   *Some* is not everybody or everything.   *Some* is a few or a bit.
   Somebody or *someone* is a person.   *Somebody* is a person whose name you do not know.
   Something is a thing.   It is anything but you do not know what.
   Sometimes is not always.   It is just now and then.
   Somewhere is one place or another but not a special place.

somersault   To *somersault* is to turn head over heels on the ground, in the air or into the water.

son   A *son* is a boy child in a family.

song   A *song* is music and words to sing.

soon   *Soon* is in a very short time.   *Soon* is not long from now.

sorry   *Sorry* is sad.   *Sorry* is not happy.   You are *sorry* when you wish you had not said or done something.

sort   What *sort* of sweets are your favourites?   What kind do you like?   Do you like all *sorts*?

To *sort* is to put things together that should be together.

sound   Anything at all you can hear with your ears is a *sound*, from a whisper to a shout, a squeak to a roar.

soup   You boil vegetables or meat or fish in water or milk to make a pot of *soup*.

sour   *Sour* is not sweet.   *Sour* is sharp, like the taste of a lemon.
Sour milk is not fresh milk.   It is old and tastes bad.

south   *South* is opposite north.   The *south* of a country is the lowest or bottom part.

space   There is nothing in *space*.
Space is empty.   There are *spaces* between your fingers and toes.
Space is room, like lots of *space* to play.
Space is the place far above the Earth where there is no air.
A *spaceship* is a special machine built to shoot up into *space*.

spade   A *spade* is a tool with a long, wide blade and a handle for digging.

spaghetti   *Spaghetti* is long strings of soft paste to twist round your fork and eat with a sauce.

sparrow   A *sparrow* is a little town bird with brown-grey feathers.

speak   To *speak* is to talk.   To *speak* is to say things for people to hear.
The wicked queen's magic mirror *spoke* words she did not want to hear.

special   *Special* is different.   *Special* is not ordinary or everyday.   Your birthday is a *special* day.
Special is made or built to do one *special* thing.
A spaceship is built *specially* for travel in space.

speed   *Speed* is how fast a thing or a person goes.   At *high speed* is very fast and *speedy*.
Hansel and Gretel *sped* from the witch's cottage as fast as they could run.

spell   When you *spell* a word you write or say its letters in the right order.

A *spell* is magic words a fairy or a witch speaks in fairy stories.
A wicked fairy's *spell* turned a prince into a frog.

spend   You *spend* money when you buy. You pay for the things you buy.

To *spend* is to pass time.
Tom Thumb *spent* a morning riding in the ear of a horse.

spider   A *spider* is a little animal with eight legs.   It *spins* a web to catch insects.

spill   If you fill a milk jug too full the milk will *spill*.   It will run over and down and all over the place.

spin   To *spin* is to turn round and round very fast like a *spinning top*.
To *spin* is to make thread out of cotton or wool or silk.   A spider *spins* its web with a silky thread from its body.
Rumpelstiltskin *spun* straw into gold with magic and a *spinning wheel*.

splash   Water flies everywhere if you jump in with a *splash*.

spoil   If you *spoil* a thing you do not look after it.   It has a scratch or a stain or a hole or a tear in it.   It might even be broken or burned like *spoiled* food.

sponge   Tiny sea animals make a soft *sponge* to wash with.   It has lots of holes in it to hold lots of water.

A *sponge* is also a soft, light cake or pudding.

spoon   You eat pudding with a *pudding spoon*, drink soup with a *soup spoon*, stir tea with a *teaspoon* and stir cooking with a *cooking spoon*.
They all have a little shallow bowl of a different size and a handle.

sport   A game is a *sport*, like football or tennis or skiing.

spot   A *spot* is a little round circle.
A *spot* is a mark or a stain.

A *spot* is a special place, like a favourite *spot* for a picnic.

To *spot* is to see.

spread   To *spread* is to lay out flat and as far as it will go, like a cloth on a table or a cover on a bed.

To *spread* is to stretch out like the branches of a tree.

To *spread* is to smooth on like butter onto bread.

spring   *Spring* is the season of the year when plants start to grow again after the cold winter.

To *spring* is to jump in the air or bounce like a ball.

A *spring* is a little stream of water flowing out of the earth.

Springs are curls of metal or wire under a bed to make it *springy*.

square   A *square* is a shape.   It has four straight sides of the same length.
A box is sometimes *square*.   A table is sometimes *square*.
A *square* in town has houses or other buildings on all four sides.

squash   To *squash* is to crush flat.   To *squash* is to squeeze.

squeak   To *squeak* is to make a little high, sharp cry like a mouse or a *squeaky* door.

squeeze   To *squeeze* is to squash or to press hard.
Oranges and lemons are *squeezed* for their juice.

squirrel   A *squirrel* is a small furry animal, red or grey with a long bushy tail.

stage   In the theatre the *stage* is the platform where players act in plays or shows and singers sing.

stain   A *stain* is a dirty mark.

stairs   *Stairs* are steps inside a building to take you *upstairs* and *downstairs*.

stalk   The *stalk* of a plant is its stem.
Leaves and flowers and ripe seeds grow from the *stalk*.

stamp   A *stamp* is stuck on a letter or parcel.   It is a little piece of coloured paper to pay for sending things by post.

If you *stamp* your foot you hit it hard on the ground.

stand   When you *stand* you are up on your feet.   You are not sitting.   You have *stood* up.

star A *star* is a bright little light seen in the clear night sky.
  A *star* is a shape with five or more points.

start To *start* is to begin. The *start* of a journey is its beginning.

station Trains start and stop at a *station*.

stay When you *stay* you do not leave. You do not go anywhere.
  To *stay* is also to make a short visit.

steal Thieves take things that do not belong to them. They *steal*.
  The wolf *stole* a ham from Tom Thumb's kitchen.

steam *Steam* rises from boiling water in a white mist.
  To *steam* is to cook with *steam*.

steel *Steel* is a very strong metal made from iron.

steep A *steep* hill is hard to climb. It rises sharply and almost straight up from the ground.

steer To *steer* is to guide a vehicle or sail a boat.

stem A *stem* is the stalk of a plant. It holds up the leaves and the flowers.

step To *step* is to walk. Your feet take you along when you *step* out.
  Steps are stairs to take you up and down one *step* at a time.

stick A *stick* is a long thin piece of wood.

To *stick* is to press down or fasten together with glue or *sticky* tape.
  Sticky is covered with glue.

still *Still* is quiet and peaceful.
  If you stand *still* you do not move.

Still means the same as before. *Still* means up until now.
  It was raining this morning and it is *still* raining now.

sting A *sting* is a sharp little pain if an insect or plant pricks your skin.

stir You *stir* tea with a teaspoon. You *stir* soup or porridge with a cooking spoon. You move the spoon round and round.

stocking A *stocking* is longer than a sock. It covers all of the leg.

stomach Your food slides down your throat into your *stomach*. It stays there until it is softer.

stone   A *stone* is a big bit or a little bit of rock.

A *stony* beach is covered in *stones* and pebbles.

A *stone* is the hard seed inside some fruits like a peach and a plum.

stool   A *stool* is a little seat with no back and no arms.   *Stools* have tall legs or short legs and some *stools* have only three legs.

stop   When things *stop* they do not go or move.

To *stop* is to finish doing what you were doing.   To *stop* is to come to an end.

The music *stopped* at the end of the tune.

A *stopper stops* a liquid from running out of a bottle.

store   To *store* is to put things away until you need them.

A squirrel *stores* nuts and seeds for the winter.

A *store* is a shop that sells nearly everything you need.

storm   The rain pours down, thunder crashes, lightning lights up the sky, a strong wind blows.   It is a *storm*. *Stormy* weather at sea whips up the waves.

story   Funny things, happy things, magic things, fearsome things can happen in a *story*.

You can listen to a *story* or read *stories* for yourself in a *storybook*.

straight   A *straight* road has no bends or curves in it.   *Straight* hair has no curls in it.

Straight is flat like a *straight* line you draw with a ruler.

Straight hair is smooth hair.

strange   *Strange* is not ordinary or usual.

A *stranger* is a person you do not know.   You have not met him or her before.

straw   *Straw* is stalks of dry wheat and oats and other grasses.

Baskets and hats are made of twisted *straw*.   Farm animals eat and sleep on *straw*.

A *straw* is a long thin tube for sucking up a drink through your lips.

strawberry   A *strawberry* is a soft, juicy red fruit covered in little seeds.

stream   A *stream* is a little flowing river.

street   A *street* is a road in town with houses or shops or other buildings on both sides.

stretch   A rubber band gets bigger and longer if you *stretch* it.

When you *stretch*, you pull yourself up tall and straight, or you lie down long and flat.

To *stretch* is also to reach for something with your arm.

strike   To *strike* is to hit hard like a nail with a hammer.

A clock *strikes* when a little hammer hits a bell.

Cinderella ran from the palace when the clock *struck* twelve.

string   *String* is thick thread to tie up things like parcels.

A *string* of beads is threaded or *strung* together to make a necklace.

strip   A *strip* is a long, flat narrow piece of anything at all.

stripe   A *stripe* is a strip of a different colour.

A zebra's coat has black and white *stripes*.   A tiger has black *stripes* on a yellow-brown body.

strong   A *strong* person and a *strong* animal can lift and carry and push and pull heavy things.   A *strong* wind can blow down trees.

Strong is not weak.   *Strong* is fit and healthy and full of *strength*.

submarine   A *submarine* is a ship that can sail under water.

suck   To *suck* is to draw something into your mouth.   You can *suck* an orange.   You can *suck* a drink through a straw.

sudden   *Sudden* is quick.   A *sudden* thing happens without warning.   It happens quickly and *suddenly*.

Suddenly Cinderella's fairy godmother stood before her.

sugar   *Sugar* is sweet.   It is rough white or brown powder to make food and drink sweet.

suit   A *suit* is a set of clothes that go together, like a jacket and trousers or a jacket and skirt.
A *suit* is also special clothes for a special job, like a *spacesuit*.

summer   *Summer* comes after spring.   It is the warmest season of the year when everything is in flower.

sun   The *sun* is the big, bright star in the sky that gives light and warmth to the Earth in the daytime.
A *sunbeam* is a ray of light or *sunshine* from the *sun*.
Sunrise is dawn when the *sun* comes up.
Sunset is the time when the *sun* goes down.

Sunday   *Sunday* is the first day of the week.

supermarket   A *supermarket* is a great big store that sells nearly everything you want to eat and drink and use at home.

supper   *Supper* is an evening meal.

sure   If you are *sure*, you know you are right.

surprise   A *surprise* is something you do not know about.   It is hard to believe it when you get a *surprise*. You are *surprised* and full of wonder.

swallow   Food and drink go down your throat when you *swallow*.

sweep   To *sweep* is to clean up with a brush, like dust on the floor or leaves in the garden.
Cinderella cleaned and *swept*.

sweet   *Sweet* is not sour.   *Sweet* is like sugar and honey and chocolate.
Sweets are all kinds of little *sweet* things made of sugar and flavours and colours.

swell   To *swell* is to grow big like a balloon full of air.

swim   You move your arms and kick your legs to *swim* through the water.

swing   To *swing* is to move gently to and fro.
A *swing* is a hanging seat that *swings* on ropes or chains from a bar or the branch of a tree.

sword   A *sword* is a weapon that strikes and cuts.   A *sword* has a long sharp blade with a point and a handle called a hilt.

T t

table   It is round or square, oval or long.   It has a flat top and legs to stand on.   It is a *table* to eat at, work at or put things on.

tadpole   A *tadpole* is a very young frog.   It has a tail and no legs yet.

tail   An animal has a long *tail*, a short *tail* or a curly *tail*.   Its *tail* grows at the end of its body.
   The *tail* of a thing is at the back or the end, like the *tail* of an aeroplane.

take   To *take* is to lift up and hold.
   To *take* is to lift up and carry from one place to another.

   To *take* is to have, like a sleep, a walk or a holiday.
   Dick Whittington's walk to London *took* a long time.   It lasted many days.

tale   A *tale* is a story in a book of *tales*.

talk   To speak is to *talk*.   You tell things when you *talk*.

tall   *Tall* is not short.   *Tall* is high like Jack's beanstalk, a giraffe and a skyscraper.

tame   *Tame* is not wild.   A *tame* animal is not afraid of people.

tank   A *tank* is a big steel car with big guns used in wars.   It moves on metal bands called tracks.

   A *tank* holds liquids and gases, like a *petrol tank.*

tap   A *tap* is a little handle to turn to get water or gas from a pipe.

   To *tap* is to pat or to knock gently.

tape   *Tape* is cloth or sticky paper in a narrow strip.
   A special kind of *tape* plays back sounds on a *tape-recorder* machine.

target   A *target* is a thing to aim at with an arrow or a gun.   It is round with smaller circles marked inside.
   A *target* can be anything you aim for or want to do.
   Dick Whittington's *target* was to get to London.

tart A *tart* is a pastry case or a pie filled with fruit or jam.

taste Your mouth and your tongue tell you what *taste* you are *tasting*. Everything you eat and drink has its own special taste.

taxi A *taxi* is a car you pay to ride in. The *taxi driver* takes your money.

tea You make *tea* when you pour boiling water on dried leaves from the *tea plant*.
  A *teapot* is a pot for *tea*. It has a lid and a handle and a thin spout to pour from.

teach To *teach* is to tell and to show how things are done.
  A *teacher* helps you to learn about all sorts of things.

team A number of people working together is a *team*.
  A number of people playing a game or a sport together is a *team*.

tear (This *tear* rhymes with hear.)
  A *tear* is a little drop of water that falls from your eye if you are sad or hurt.
  In tears means to cry.

tear (This *tear* rhymes with hair.)
  A *tear* is a long hole. If you catch your sleeve on a sharp point it *tears*.
  Paper is easily *torn* into pieces with your fingers.

telephone Your voice is carried far away by electric wires when you speak on the *telephone*.
  The *telephone* is the instrument you lift to speak into and answer when it rings.

telescope A *telescope* brings things far away close up to your eye.
  It is a long tube to look through with special glass and mirrors inside.

television Like a little cinema at home, a *television* brings pictures and sounds through the air by electricity.

tell To *tell* is to say things.
  To *tell is* to give people news or *tell* them a tale.
  The wicked queen's magic mirror *told* her Snow White was more beautiful than she.

ten *Ten* is 10. It is one more than nine. You have *ten* fingers and *ten* toes.
  Ten times *ten* is one hundred.

tennis *Tennis* is a game played with *tennis rackets*. A soft ball is hit to and fro across a *tennis net*.

tent You camp and sleep in a *tent* out of doors.
  A *tent* is made of strong cloth and held up by poles and ropes.

terrible   *Terrible* is fearsome.   *Terrible* is bad and not pleasant at all.

thank   '*Thank* you for letting me go to the ball,' Cinderella said to her fairy godmother.
   She *thanked* her because she was pleased and glad.

theatre   A *theatre* is a building where players act on the stage in plays and shows and singers sing.

there   *There* is not here.   *There* is not in this place.   It is in that place.
   There is where you are going when you travel.   You have got *there* when you arrive.

thick   *Thick* is not thin.   *Thick* is wide and fat, like the trunk of a tree.
   Thick porridge is not thin and flowing.
   Thick is strong and heavy, like a *thick* overcoat.
   Thick is deep, like *thick* snow.

thief   A *thief* steals things that do not belong to him.   He *thieves* and he robs.   *Thieves* are robbers.

thin   *Thin* is not thick or fat or wide. *Thin* is narrow and fine.

thing   A *thing* is something or anything at all that is not alive.
   If you do not know what something is called you can call it a *thing*.

think   You use your mind when you *think*.
   To *think* is also to believe something is true.
   Red Riding Hood *thought* the wicked wolf was her grandmother.

thirsty   You want to drink when you are *thirsty*.   Your mouth is dry.   Your throat is dry.
   You have a *thirst*.

thousand   A *thousand* is 1000.   A *thousand* is ten times one hundred.

thread   A long thin *thread* is spun from cotton or silk.
   Thread is *threaded* into a needle to sew and to mend.

three   *Three* is 3.   It is one more than two.
   Thirteen is 13.   Ten and *three* make *thirteen*.
   Thirty is 30. *Thirty* is ten times *three*.

thrill   A *thrill* is a quick, happy, excited feeling.   You are *thrilled* and full of joyful excitement.

throat   Inside the front of your neck is your *throat*.
   You breathe air and swallow food down your *throat*.

throne   A *throne* is a large grand chair for a king or a queen to sit on.

through   From one side to the other is *through*.
You pass *through* a doorway.
You look *through* a window.

throw   You send a thing fast through the air when you *throw* it from your hand.
Jack's mother *threw* the magic beans into the garden. She tossed them out.

thumb   Your *thumb* is your first finger. It is shorter and thicker than your other fingers.

thunder   In a storm *thunder* is the loud crack or growling noise in the sky after a flash of lightning.

Thursday   *Thursday* is the fifth day of the week.

ticket   A train *ticket*, a bus *ticket*, a theatre *ticket* – they are all little pieces of paper or card you buy to let you go somewhere.

tickle   A light stroke or a dig with the fingers will *tickle* and make you laugh.

tidy   *Tidy* is neat, with everything in its own place.
Snow White *tidied* the Seven Dwarfs' little house.

tie   To *tie* is to fasten with string or thread or ribbon.
You *tie* a *tie* in a knot or a bow under your collar.

tiger   A *tiger* is a big dangerous wild cat with a yellow-brown body and black stripes.   It lives in the forests in hot lands.

tight   *Tight* is not loose.   A *tight* lid on a tin box fits closely.
The wicked queen *tightened* the ribbon round Snow White's waist so *tightly* she could not breathe.

Tights are two stockings in one piece fitting the legs *tightly*.

time   *Time* is marked in years, months, weeks, days, hours, minutes and seconds.
You read the *time* of day or night on a clock or a watch.
Time is how long it takes to do a thing.
Time is a special hour of the day like *breakfast time*.
Time is a special day of the year like *Christmas time*.

tin   *Tin* is a soft silver-white metal.
A *tin* is a can to hold all sorts of things from paint to peas.

tiny   *Tiny* is very, very, small, like Tom Thumb.   He was only the size of his mother's thumb.

tip   The *tip* is the thin end of a thing, like the *tip* of your nose or your *fingertips*.
   The *tip* is the sharp point of a thing, like a pin or *a* pen.

To *tip* is to upset or knock over.

tired   If you are *tired* you need to rest or to sleep.
   If you are *tired* of one thing try something different.

to   If you go *to* a place you go on and towards it.
   To and fro is from side to side or up and down like a swinging swing.

toast   Heat a slice of bread till it is nice and brown and crisp and it is *toast*.

today   This day is *today*.   At this moment you are living in *today*.

toe   A *toe* is part of your foot.   One foot has five *toes*.   Two feet have ten *toes*.

together   Strawberries and cream are nice *together*.   They go with each other.
   The Seven Dwarfs all lived *together* in their little house.   They lived with each other.

tomato   A *tomato* is a red or yellow fruit.   It is soft and juicy with a sharp fresh taste.

tomorrow   *Tomorrow* is the day after today.   When *tomorrow* comes it will be today.

tongue   Your *tongue* is pink and soft and thick and moves about in your mouth.   You need your *tongue* to talk and taste and lick and eat with.

tonight   *Tonight* is this night.   It will be *tonight* when today is over.

too   *Too* is also. *Too* is as well.
   Too much is more than enough. It is more than you want.

tool   A hammer is a *tool*.   An axe, a saw, a spade, a rake are *tools*.
   Tools make and fix and do all sorts of jobs.

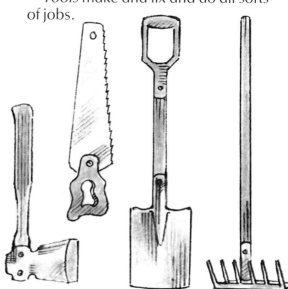

tooth   A *tooth* is one of the white bones in your mouth you bite and eat with.   You have two rows of *teeth*.
  Some tools have *teeth*, like a saw for sawing.

top   The *top* of a hill is the highest part.
  The *top* of the stairs is as high as you can go.
  The *top* of a tube or a bottle is a little lid to close at the *top*.

  A toy *top* spins round very fast on the floor.

torch   A *torch* or a *flashlight* is a little lamp you can hold.   You press a button to get a long thin ray of light.

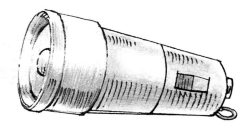

toss   To *toss* is to throw high in the air.

touch   To *touch* is to feel or to tap with the tips of your fingers.
  Your *touch* tells you if a thing is hot or cold, wet or dry, hard or soft.
  If things *touch* each other there is no space between, like books on a shelf.

tough   *Tough* is strong and thick.
  Tough is hard.   *Tough* is not cooked enough, like *tough* meat.

towards   You keep on going on when you go *towards* a thing or a place.
  You go forward.

towel   A *towel* dries you when you are wet.   It is made of good thick cloth.

tower   A *tower* is tall and square or tall and round.   It stands high on its own or at the top of a castle or a church.
  Rapunzel was kept in a *tower* till her hair was as long as the *tower* was high.

town   A *town* is a busy place full of buildings and streets and people. It is not so big as a city, but bigger than a village.

toy   A *toy* is something to play with.   A top, a scooter, a kite, a doll, a train set are all *toys* to have fun with.

track   The *track* is the rails for trains to run on.
  A *track* is a rough path to walk on.
  Your feet mark a *track* on wet sand.   Animals too leave their *tracks* on the ground.

tractor   A *tractor* is a big heavy machine with fat tyres.   It pulls heavy loads.
  A *tractor* on the farm pulls the plough and farm wagons.

traffic   Cars and buses and trucks and every other moving vehicle make the *traffic* on streets and roads and highways.

Ships and aeroplanes are sea *traffic* and air *traffic*.

A *traffic warden* looks after *traffic* and car parking in town.

train   A *train* is an engine with coaches behind full of people or wagons full of heavy loads. A *train* travels on the railway track.

To *train* is to learn.
To *train* is to keep fit with exercises.
A *trainer* helps to make good sportsmen and women.

travel   When you *travel* you go from one place to another.

To *travel* is to make a journey on foot or by road or sea or air.

treasure   Rich and precious things are *treasure*, like gold and silver and jewels.

Your *treasures* are the things you love and want to keep safe for ever.

tree   A *tree* is a plant that grows tall on its trunk.   Branches shooting like arms from the trunk are leafy and green in spring and summer.

trick   It is clever, it is funny, it is surprising, it looks like magic.   It is a *trick*.

trip   A *trip* is a short little journey, like a *trip* to the zoo or a *day trip* to the sea.

You *trip* when you catch your toe and nearly fall over.

trouble   *Trouble* is something difficult that makes people worry and feel unhappy.

trousers   *Trousers* start at your waist and end at your ankles and cover your legs in between.

truck   A *truck* or a lorry is a big heavy motor vehicle that carries heavy loads.

true   *True* is right and good and real and straight.

The *truth* is *true* things and *true* words.   It is not lies and stories.

trumpet   A *trumpet* is a musical instrument.   It is shaped like a bell at one end and makes lovely loud music when the *trumpeter* blows it.

trunk   The *trunk* of a tree is the thick wood stem it stands on.

An elephant's *trunk* is its long nose.

A *trunk* is a big, strong, heavy box to keep or to carry clothes on a journey.

try   You work hard to do something when you *try*. If you do not do it first time you *try* again.

The wicked wolf *tried* and *tried to* blow down the Little Pig's house of bricks.

T-shirt　A *T-shirt* is a thin, light cotton shirt.

tub　A tub is made of wood or metal, wide and open at the top. You can wash in a *tub* or store things in a *tub*.
　A *tub* is a bath.
　A little paper *tub* with a lid holds things like ice cream and butter.

tube　A *tube* is anything long and thin and empty inside, like a drinking straw or a pipe.
　A *tube* is also a small soft bottle to squeeze, like a *tube* of toothpaste.

Tuesday　*Tuesday* is the third day of the week.

tug　To *tug* is to pull and pull, like the old man who could not pull his giant turnip out of the ground.

A *tug* is a little boat with a strong engine that pulls big ships out of harbour.

You pull hard on a rope in a game of *tug o' war*.

tumble　To *tumble* is to fall or roll or twist.
　To *tumble* is to turn head over heels in a somersault.

tumbler　A *tumbler* is a clever *tumbling* acrobat.

A *tumbler* is a tall glass to drink from.

tune Musical notes follow one after another to make a *tune* to play or sing.

The Pied Piper's *tuneful* pipe brought all the rats from their holes.

tunnel A *tunnel* is a long hole dug through a hill or under a river or under the ground.

Trains and cars pass through *tunnels*.

turkey A *turkey* is a big bird with no feathers on its head or its neck.

The *turkey cock* has a big colourful tail.

turn To *turn* is to go round and round like a wheel or a top.

To *turn* is to go back along the way you came.

If you *turn* your head you look to one side or the other, or behind you.

To *turn into* is to change or become something else.

Before Puss in Boots' eyes, the giant *turned into* a mouse.

turnip A turnip is a round root vegetable, little or large, yellow or white, to eat when cooked.

twelve *Twelve* is 12. It is one more than eleven. *Twelve o'clock* in the daytime is noon or midday.

Twelve o'clock at night is midnight.

twenty *Twenty* is 20. *Twenty* is twice ten.

twice *Twice* is two times.

twig A *twig* is a very little branch on a big branch of a tree.

twin If you have a *twin* you have a brother or sister who was born at the same time as you.

twist To *twist* is to turn or to spin.

To *twist* is to change shape like a tree trunk *twisted* by the wind.

two *Two* is 2. It is one more than one.

Two is a pair, like a pair of gloves for your *two* hands.

type A *type* is a sort or a kind.

Chocolate is one *type* of sweet.

To *type* is to tap the keys on a *typewriter* and print words on paper.

tyre A *tyre* is a thick circle of rubber round the outside of a wheel.

ugly Cinderella's *ugly* sisters were not beautiful to look at.

umbrella You hold an *umbrella* above your head on rainy days. It is cloth pulled tight over thin rods that slide up and down a long stick in the middle.

uncle An *uncle* is the brother of your mother or father.

under *Under* is below. *Under* is not on top. You wear *underclothes underneath* your other clothes.

understand You know what things mean if you *understand* them.

undo When you *undo* buttons, zips, shoelaces and knots, they are not fastened or tied or closed. They are *undone*.

undress You take off your clothes when you *undress*.

uniform A *uniform* is special clothes for a special job.
Nurses, policemen, soldiers, sailors wear their own *uniforms*.
Do you wear school *uniform*?

untidy The opposite of neat and tidy is *untidy*. Things are all over the place and it is a mess.

until The Frog Prince was not a prince *until* the princess kissed him. Up to that moment he was a frog.

up Jack climbed *up* the beanstalk. He went from the bottom to the top.
When you go *upstairs* from downstairs you go *up* from the floor below.

upon *Upon* is the same as on. *Upon* is on top and not underneath.

upset To *upset* is to tip, to turn or knock over or to spill.

If you are *upset* you are not very happy and maybe not very well.

upside down Wrong way up is *upside down*.
Stand on your head with your feet in the air and you are *upside down*.

use You *use* a comb to comb your hair, a hammer to hammer a nail. The comb and the hammer do the things they are made for doing. They have a *use*. They are *useful* and helpful and handy.
Useless things are not helpful. They do not work. They are broken or worn out.

usual It is *usual* to sleep in a bed. It is nearly always done.

Usual is not special or different. *Usual* is ordinary.

Usually is not always but almost every time.

V v

vacant   *Vacant* is empty.   There is nothing and nobody in a *vacant* house.

vacuum   *Vacuum* is emptiness. *Vacuum* is empty space.
   A *vacuum cleaner* is an electric machine that sucks up dirt and dust.

valuable   *Valuable* is precious. *Valuable* things are of great *value*. They are worth a lot of money, like jewels and things made of silver and gold.
   Valuable is important.

van   A *van* is a covered truck for carrying things from place to place.   A *mail van* carries letters and parcels.

   A *van* is a caravan.

vanish   To *vanish* is to disappear suddenly from sight.

vase   A *vase* is a pot for holding flowers in water.

vegetable   A *vegetable* is any plant that is not a fruit grown to be eaten.

vehicle   A *vehicle* moves and carries people and things from one place to another.

very   *Very* good is more than good.   It is specially good.
   Very bad is more than bad.   It is specially bad.

vest   You wear a *vest* under your clothes and next to your skin on the top part of your body.

vet   A *vet* takes care of animals when they are sick or hurt.
   Vet is a short word for *veterinary surgeon* or *veterinarian*.

It's a **very** busy day at the **vet's**.

victory A *victory* is won in a game or a fight by the best player, the best team or the best army.

They do not lose.   They are the *victors*.

video recorder A *video recorder* makes and plays tapes to show on a television screen.

village A *village* is a very small, quiet town.

vine Grapes grow on a *vine*.   Some *vines* climb as they grow, some grow along the ground.

violet A *violet* is a little springtime plant with blue-purple or white flowers.

Violet is a light blue-purple colour.

violin A *violin* is a musical instrument with strings.

The *violinist* holds it under his chin and plays on the strings with a stick called a bow.

visit You go to see someone when you *visit*.   You stay for a short time.

voice You speak, you sing, you make sounds with your *voice*.   Your lips move when you use your *voice*.

volcano A *volcano* is a mountain. Now and then, hot ash and liquid rocks, dust and gases burst from a hole, or crater, at the top and pour down the mountain side.

W w

wagon   A farmer has a four-wheeled *wagon* to carry heavy loads.   A tractor pulls the *wagon* along.
A *wagon* is a truck on the road or the railway.

waist   Your *waist* is the middle of your body.   Trousers and skirts hang from the *waist*.

wait   You stay where you are when you *wait*.
You are *waiting* for something to happen or for somebody to come along.
Jack *waited* in the oven until the giant fell asleep.

waiter   In a restaurant or a hotel, a *waiter* or *waitress* brings food to your table.

wake   You open your eyes.   You are not asleep any more when you *wake*.

walk   Your feet carry you along when you *walk*.   You step out.

wall   A *wall* is built of bricks or stone or wood.
A *wall* is one side of a house.
Buildings need *walls* to stand.
A *wall* is put up like a fence round a building, a garden or a park.

want   What do you *want* most of all? What would you like and wish for and hope to have?

war   A *war* is a fight between countries. A *war* is a fight between people.

warm   *Warm* is not too hot.   It is nicely hot.
On a *warm* day you feel the *warmth* of the sun.
To *warm* food you heat it gently.

warn   To *warn* is to tell someone to be careful or to watch out for danger.
A *warning* sign is a danger sign.

wash   To *wash* is to make clean with water or with soap and water – yourself, the dishes, clothes or anything at all that is dirty.

wasp   A *wasp* is a flying, stinging insect with black and yellow stripes like a bee.
It is thinner than a bee and does not make honey.

waste   *Waste* is rubbish and useless things to throw in the dustbin or the *waste basket*.

If you *waste*, you use too much or spend too much money. You are not careful enough.

watch   To *watch* is to look at.
Cinderella worked and the lazy ugly sisters *watched*.

To *watch* is to look after, like a *watchdog*.

To *watch out* is to be careful.

A *watch* is a little clock to wear on your wrist.

water *Water* falls as rain from the clouds.

Water runs in rivers. *Water* fills the sea, the lakes, the ponds.

Water is wet, *water* is clear. You can drink it, wash in it, swim in it, sail on it.

waterproof *Waterproof* things keep out the water and keep you dry.

Raincoats and umbrellas are *waterproof*.

wave A *wave* is a rolling curve of water on the sea. The stronger the wind, the bigger the *waves*.

Flags *wave* in the wind. They float and shake to and fro.

You stretch and *wave* your arm to and fro when you call goodbye.

wax *Wax* is the thick, soft, fatty material candles are made of.

Bees make their own *wax* for their honey.

way A *way* is a road or a path or a highway.

The *way* also means what to do and how to do a thing.

Do you know the *way* to whistle a tune?

weak *Weak* is not strong, like a thin little branch that bends and breaks.

weapon Any instrument used for fighting is a *weapon*, like a gun or a sword.

wear You put on the clothes you *wear*. You carry them on your body.

Summer *wear* is worn in summer.

To *wear* is also to *wear* too much or to use things too long. They are old and holey and useless and *worn out*.

weather What the air outside is like from day to day is the *weather*.

It can be hot or cold or wet or dry or a little bit of all of them.

web A *web* is a fine silky net spiders spin to catch insects to eat.

Some swimming birds and animals have *webbed feet*. Their toes are joined together by skin.

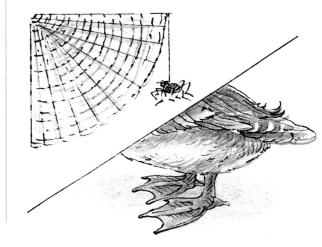

wedding At a *wedding* a man and a woman marry to become husband and wife.

Wednesday *Wednesday* is the fourth day of the week. *Wednesday* is the middle of the week.

weed A *weed* is a plant growing wild. Too many *weeds* in the garden need *weeding* out but lots of *weeds* have pretty flowers.

week A *week* is seven days from Sunday to Saturday.

weep Tears fall from your eyes when you *weep* because you are sad.
   The princess *wept* when she lost her golden ball.

weigh You find out how heavy you are when you *weigh* yourself on the scales.
   Little numbers tell you your *weight*.

well You are fit. You are healthy. You are *well*.
   You do *well* when you do a good job.

west The *west* is where the sun goes down at sunset?
   The *west* is opposite the east.

wet *Wet* is not dry. You get *wet* in the bath. You get *wet* in the rain. You are covered in water.

whale The *whale* is the biggest animal of all. It lives in the sea and breathes through a hole in the top of its head called a blowhole.

wheat *Wheat* is a tall grass. Its ripe seeds are crushed to make flour.

wheel A *wheel* is round. It is made of metal or wood and turns as it moves.
   A *wheelbarrow* has two handles to hold and rolls along on one *wheel* when you push it.

when *When* do you eat? *When* do you sleep? *When* do you do anything at all?
   When is the time that you do things.

where *Where* do you eat? *Where* do you sleep? *Where* do you do anything at all?
   Where is the place that you do things.

whisper You speak very softly when you *whisper*. You do not want everybody to hear.

whistle You can *whistle* if you blow through your mouth or your teeth with your lips nearly closed.
   You make a high, tuneful sound or a high, sharp cry.
   A *whistle* is a special little pipe you blow to make the same sounds.

white *White* is the colour of snow. *White* things are not coloured.

whole   *Whole* is all.   It is not just a bit or a part, it is all of a thing.
Goldilocks ate all Baby Bear's porridge.   She ate the *whole* bowlful.

wicked   *Wicked* is very bad, like the wicked wolf who swallowed Red Riding Hood's grandmother.

wide   *Wide* is not thin or narrow.   *Wide* is big and broad and a long way from side to side, like the sea.
Your mouth is open *wide* when you yawn.

wife   A *wife* is a woman who has married.
Cinderella became the *wife* of the prince.

wig   A *wig* is a covering of hair to put on the head.   A *wig* covers a bald head.
Wigs cover actors' heads when they want to look different.

wigwam   A *wigwam* is a tent of poles covered in animal skins or grasses or wood from the outside of tree trunks.
American Indians once lived in *wigwams*.

wild   *Wild* animals live in the fields, the woods, the jungle.   They are not tame and do not live with people.
The *wild* is country far from towns and people.

win   To *win* is to come first in a race or a battle.   To *win* is to beat all the others.
A *winner* gets first prize for being clever at anything at all.

wind   *Wind* is air blowing hard and strong or lightly and gently all around us.
The arms or the sails of a *windmill* are turned by the *wind* to make wheat into flour.

wind   (This *wind* rhymes with find.)
To *wind* is to twist and curl and turn round and round or in and out, like a *winding* road.
To *wind* is to turn a little *winder* or a key in a clock.   Clocks are *wound* to keep them going.

window   A *window* is a sheet of glass to let in the daylight.
If you are inside you look through a *window* to see outside.

wing   A *wing* is one of a bird's feathery arms that let it fly in the air.
Insects have little silky *wings*.
Aeroplanes have strong metal *wings* for flying.

winter   *Winter* is the coldest season of the year, when trees have no buds or leaves and daylight is short.

wipe   To *wipe* is to rub or clean lightly or dry with a cloth or a towel.

wire   *Wire* is metal in a fine, thin strip.

Which is the **witch** and which is the **wizard**?

wise   *Wise* people think and understand and know many things.
They have *wisdom.*

wish   To *wish* is to want a thing very much.
Cinderella's *wish* came true when she went to the ball.

witch   In stories a *witch* is an ugly old woman who makes magic spells. She wears a tall, black pointed hat and flies through the air on a broomstick.

with   Cups go *with* saucers.   Hansel goes *with* Gretel.   They go together.
If you are *with* someone or *with* others, you are not by yourself.

You eat *with* a fork.   You see *with* your eyes.   They are the things you use.

without   If you are *without* a thing you do not have it.
Jack was sent to bed *without* any supper.   He had none.

wizard   In stories a *wizard* is a man who makes magic spells, good or bad.

wolf   A *wolf* is a wild animal that looks like a dog.

woman   A *woman* is a girl who has grown up.   *Women* are adult females.

wonder   You want to know when you *wonder.*   You are excited about finding out.
Jack *wondered* what he would find at the top of the beanstalk.   Would it be something *wonderful* and surprising and marvellous?

wood   *Wood* is the trunk of trees.
Wood is sawed and cut and shaped to make lots of *wooden* things.
A *wood* is trees all growing together like a small forest.

wool   The thick *woolly* coat of a sheep is cut and spun into *wool* for warm *woollen* clothes and rugs and carpets.

word A *word* is a sound you say and understand.

You write the letters in a *word* and read the *word* and know what the *word* means.

work You are doing a job when you *work*. You are busy. You are not playing.

world The *world* is all the earth and sky. It is everybody and everything.

worm A *worm* is a little animal with no legs. It twists and slides in and out of the earth like a very small snake.

worry You are not very happy when you *worry*. You have trouble. Things are not easy to do and you are *worried*.

worse It was bad when the wicked wolf blew down the first Little Pig's house.

It was *worse* when it blew down the second Little Pig's house. It was more wicked.

Red Riding Hood's wolf was the *worst* wolf of all. He was the most wicked one.

worth Gold and jewels are *worth* a lot of money. They are valuable and precious.

wrap You *wrap* parcels and presents. You cover them up with paper.

If it is cold, you can *wrap* yourself in something warm. You put it round you to cover yourself up.

wrist Your *wrist* is the thin part of your arm between your hand and your elbow.

A *wristwatch* is worn round the *wrist*.

write You draw letters and words and numbers on paper when you *write*. You *write* with a pen or a pencil and can read what you have *written*.

wrong *Wrong* is not right. If you are *wrong* you have made a mistake.

Wrong is not good or true.

If something is *wrong* with an engine it is not working well.

If something is *wrong* with you, you may not feel well.

x-ray   An *x-ray* is a special ray that takes pictures of the inside of the body.

xylophone   A *xylophone* is a musical instrument of wooden bars that play tunes when hit with two hammers.

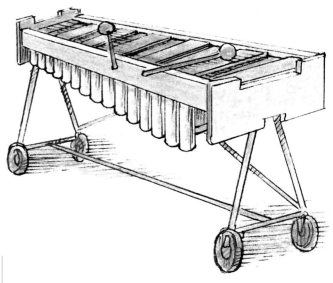

yacht   A *yacht* is a boat that races over the water with the wind in its sails.
   Some *yachts* have motors and no sails.

yard   A *yard* is a place inside a fence or inside a wall outside a house.
   A *yard* is sometimes a garden.

yawn   You *yawn*; you breathe in and your mouth opens wide.   You *yawn* because you are sleepy or maybe tired of doing what you are doing.

year   A *year* is twelve months from January to December.
   A *year* is fifty-two weeks or 365 days.

yell   To *yell* is to shout and scream and give loud cries.

yellow   *Yellow* is the colour of daffodils and bananas.

yesterday   *Yesterday* is the day before today.

yet   *Yet* is still.   *Yet* is up until now or up until then.
   Goldilocks was not *yet* awake when the Bears came home.   She was still asleep.

yoghurt or **yogurt**   *Yoghurt* is thick milk with a nice sour taste.

young   *Young* is not old.   *Young* is new like *young* leaves or a new baby.
   Are you the *youngest* in age in your family, or is someone *younger* than you?

yo-yo   A *yo-yo* is a round toy on a string.   Up and down and to and fro you can spin it with the end of the string in a loop round your finger.

Z z

zebra   A *zebra* is a wild animal like a horse with black and white stripes.

zebra crossing   A strip of road painted with black and white stripes is a *zebra crossing*.
   You can walk across a road safely on a *zebra crossing*.

Goodness! A **zebra's** crossing on the **zebra crossing**!
How did it escape from the **zoo**?

zero   *Zero* is nothing.   *Zero* is 0.

zigzag   A *zigzag* line is not a straight line.   It goes in and out in sharp bends from side to side.

zip   A *zip* is a long fastener for clothes or for bags.
   Little teeth come together as it slides up to close.

zoo   A *zoo* is a big animal park.   You can see all sorts of animals from all over the world at a *zoo*.